Pigs Eat Wolves

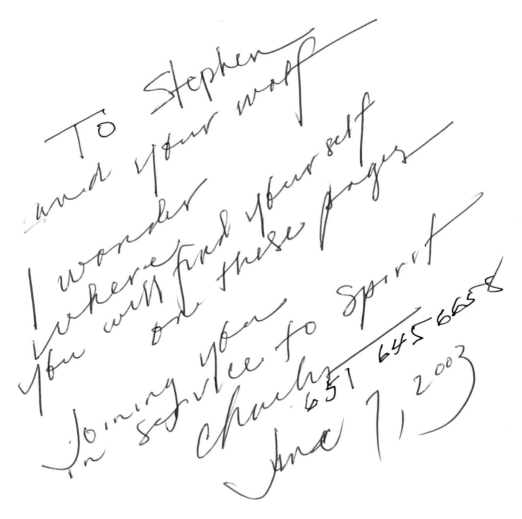

To Stephen
and your wolf
I wonder
where you will find yourself
on these pages

Joining you
in service to spirit
Chuck
651 645 6658
June 7, 2003

PIGS EAT WOLVES
GOING INTO PARTNERSHIP
WITH YOUR DARK SIDE

Charles Bates

Afterword by Robert Bly
Illustrated by Mike McColl

YES INTERNATIONAL PUBLISHERS
St. Paul, Minnesota

Library of Congress Cataloging in Publication Data
Bates, Charles, 1942–
Pigs eat wolves: going into partnership with your dark side /
Charles Bates; illustrated by Mike McColl.
    p.   cm.
Includes bibliographical references.
ISBN 0-936663-26-x
1. Maturation (Psychology) 2. Shadow (Psychoanalysis)
2. Personality and culture. 4. Three little pigs.
I Title.
bf710.b38 1991
155.2'5 – dc20
91-12072
CIP

Printed in the United States of America

To my teacher,
the wolf in my life.

Acknowledgments

The contributions of my teacher, to whom this book is dedicated, extend far beyond words. He has left me unfettered, and at the same time, has shown me a guiding love out of which I continually draw strength and courage.

I warmly acknowledge the brotherly nurturing of Robert Bly who took time from his own writing to read and reread this manuscript, give me his encouragement and feedback, and write the inspiring last pages of this book.

Many thanks to my esteemed colleague, Charlie Seashore, for his enthusiastic support and his compelling invitation to the readers of these pages.

During the course of my career there have been many, far too numerous to mention, who have contributed to my thinking and personal growth. Special thanks, however, goes to the Dr. John Carter and the Gestalt Institute of Cleveland's Organizational and Systems Development staff for modeling their clarity and impeccable thinking process.

Special appreciation to Dr. Justin O'Brien (Swami Jaidev) for his invaluable suggestions and to Mike McColl for his brilliant illustrations.

Finally, a special thanks to Theresa, whose questions, criticism, suggestions, and long hours of rewriting with me have been invaluable in making this book what it is.

INTRODUCTION

I ASSUME Jung has been paying close attention to recent developments that elaborate and expand some of the key concepts he has sponsored in our quest to understand our human condition. I am sure he is amused to see that not even The Three Little Pigs has escaped our attention in looking for ways to explore the concept of the shadow, or dark side, of our nature. Little did we know when we heard and reheard the telling of this story that each of us turns out to incorporate not only all three of those little pigs but the big bad wolf as well.

The compelling nature of childhood stories and fairy tales is evident again through the power of myth and symbol. Our intrigue is warranted by the power of these stories to excite our consciousness but also to penetrate into a deeper and more primitive level of our being that may escape our awareness.

Pigs Eat Wolves challenges us to accept, as part of our being, those characteristics which we would like to see only in others. We embody the naïve and wishful thinking, the dutiful and plodding sense of responsibility taking, the cautious and fearful wondering, and the outrageous and unpredictable violent side of life. To see and accept within ourselves the full range of our humanity is all that is asked by this enlightening, entertaining, shocking, and delightful recasting of this classic tale.

Charles Bates takes a small number of clearly written pages, with delightful and provocative illustrations, to help us see our total self, the light and the dark, and the gradations in between. If you do not want to be disturbed by this challenge, don't risk reading this book. It says it over and over in different ways: we prefer to project onto others those things we find difficult within ourselves. But it is only an illusory sense of peace that comes from pushing away the difficult sides of self.

Empowerment comes from our openness to all aspects of our nature. Denial leads to much pain, in ourselves and others. Accepting the nurturing, loving mother pig in ourselves is as difficult for some of us as it is for others to come to terms with the big bad wolf.

All this book asks is that we give up the illusion that most, if not all, goodness resides within us and most, if not all, evil exists outside us. A powerful message for a small book.

CHARLIE SEASHORE, PH.D.
Past Chairman, National Training Laboratories
Faculty, Fielding Institute, Santa Barbara, CA

Preface

WE ALL GREW UP on fairy tales, their telling ransomed from parent, teacher, or babysitter with promise of quiet or sleep. Our minds then imagined whole new worlds into existence – worlds richly populated with fantastic creatures, heroic feelings, colorful settings.

From fairy tales we learned that good triumphs over evil, purity comes through innocence, cleverness pays, valor is noble, and princes and princesses are always beautiful. Each of these lessons was summoned from our deep unconscious, or profoundly planted there.

Fairy tale, myth, and theater have served the human community in conveying teachings, giving meaning, preserving history, and foretelling the future. The storyteller renders fables, legends, and gossip – stories familiar and foreign – to all ears that listen. Remolded by custom and the needs of the time, each tale passes through the voice of the teller, chronicling social evolution and bearing the imprint of each community's need.

Today, more than ever, we need fairy tales. They have value for us both as children and as adults. The child in us listens in wonder and the adult we have become brings mature experience to the reading. In retelling the stories of our childhood, we go back to the ground of our experience, creating the opportunity to look at ourselves in new ways.

The global community searches for its own maturity as it moves round and round life's carousel. Seeking an unexplored depth in the community soul, seeking leaders moved by a call to compassion, justice, and reflection, seeking their own transformation, men and women reach out to grasp the brass ring for the next ride. Fairy tales and myth are the music that gives rhythm, meaning, and excitement to the ride; they are the metaphors and poetry of the human psyche.

The story of The Three Little Pigs is just such a metaphor. It is a map, and its analysis provides an insightful look at human nature. The metaphor is much more than a map, however; it is the terrain itself. Metaphor provides a rich learning environment. When used to model the experience of self-discovery, it provides us the opportunity to observe the larger patterns, analyze the intricacies of behavior, and foresee the obstacles we will encounter in that experience.

Along my way, the fable of The Three Little Pigs has provided me with images that help make meaning of my journey. Through the story, I have come to understand that I am the little pigs as I move through the stages of human development they each represent. I also learned that community and culture, like Mother Pig, have raised me on their stories of life and defined who I am while nurturing me. Most of all, I found that I am often eaten by the wolf.

Life has made it clear that if I am to gain any mastery of myself, my lessons are to be found and contacted inside the arenas I avoid. Knowledge continues to demand that I lift mastery out of the open hands of what I fear.

Meeting the most dangerous person in my life, my spiritual teacher, marked the formal beginning of my journey. He was a conscious wolf who pulled me along the path while making it look as if he was chasing me, paradoxically devouring me when he was nurturing me.

This book evolved out of my understanding of what I have learned. By being pressed against the edges of personal boundaries, I have experienced the essential role of paradox in giving dimension, mystery, and richness to life. Paradox demands that I seek and embrace wholes rather that horde parts as I stumble, walk, and run along the path.

The Three Little Pigs shares a motif used by many cultures under a variety of names. The Italians tell the tale of The Three Goslings; the Africans relate The Tiny Pig; in Turkey the story is told as The Three Hares; and from the French we get The Three Pullets. You may be familiar with only the shortened form of its telling, ending with the wolf's defeat at the brick house. This abridged story robs us of the important lessons of the third pig's trials and his resulting maturation. Some modern editions would have us believe that all the pigs survive the wolf, but that portrayal levels the magnificent structure of systematic human development, including failure, and does us all a disservice. *Pigs Eat Wolves* uses the full version of the story because that version provides us with profound insights into ourselves and a vision for a compelling future.

There are many sides of ourselves that we deny. We are frightened or repulsed by them and do not want to admit them into awareness. For ensuring our survival, we develop protective structures to defend against the power in those denied sides. We bury that power in the darkness, called the unconscious, and there we try to keep it safely out of sight. Our culture, too, tells us what is to be ignored, what is not to be done, and what is wrong. We dutifully store these forbidden areas in the darkness as well.

A time comes in our development when we need to take back what we and our culture have put into the darkness because some of what we have buried there is essential for our next steps.

The story of The Three Little Pigs is a story about that taking back. A tale of an ever-maturing truth, it is full of symbols: the mother represents culture; the wolf personifies the darkness; the three pigs typify the levels of development; the events enact moments and methods of integration.

This is a story of the seeker's quest — a venture into the darkness of the unknown. All of the characters, objects, and actions in the story are you. Attend to this story with care, for the story told is your own.

CB

I

LIFE WITH MOTHER

ONCE UPON A TIME *there were three little pigs. They lived with their mother in a happy home in the middle of a peaceful glen. ❨ After breakfast of porridge, mother pig usually worked in the house and garden while the little pigs frolicked and played as much as they liked. ❨ At midday the pigs protected themselves from the sun by rolling in the cool mud on the bank of the stream that ran through their yard. ❨ Life was happy for the little pigs and they thought it would always be so.*

THE THREE LITTLE PIGS are just like us – from the time we enter life until the time we begin our route to maturity.

We're all naïve at the beginning. Personal circumstances of life then intervene to mature us slowly and carefully or else push us roughly into the face of stark reality. While circumstances differ, the same patterns of human development are shared by all of us. We all stand at various stages of growth. Where we stand defines what we see and determines the way we make sense of the world.

Each of the three little pigs represents stages of development common to all of us. They show our struggles as we pass through each stage in order to mature. In the maturing process, all of us develop and affirm ourselves through a ceaseless and complex interweaving of our environment and our inner growth. Like us, the pigs learn that life unfolds in relationship, is tested in relationship, and ultimately matures in relationship.

You might find yourself in all three of these pigs as the story unfolds, yet one pig will probably predominate in your life.

The first pig seems frivolous, the second pig wants to do everything just right, the third pig is smart but is bound by habitual defense patterns. They are all naïve as they begin their quests as impotent innocents. Life will serve as a theater for the little pigs to act out respective stages of development and eventually, in the person of the third pig, outgrow innocence. If the pigs survive, they will be initiated into a new definition of self-empowered with new maturity; if they don't, they will be consumed by what they continually ignore or fear.

STAGES OF LIFE

In the art and science of fairy tale analysis, the tale of the little pigs is referred to as an "elder tale." This is shown by the story's focus on the eldest pig, which represents the later stages of life. The story, however, is not only for the middle aged and elders. Its truths are real for all those who can understand them. Its call, though, will appear undeniable and pressing at the middle and later stages of life.

In fables and myths where the youngest win the prize of enlightenment, the quest is gained through innocence and naïveté. In the stories where the eldest wins the prize of enlightenment, the quest is gained through maturity. In this case the story serves us as a map, guiding each seeker through the stages of human psychological and transformative spiritual development.

GENDER OF THE PIGS

Fables and myths are everyone's stories. In this tale, the gender of the pigs serves to tell us which aspect of the psyche is being designated and mapped for development. In that mapping, cultural preferences will resolve the meaning and the method of questioning that determine the direction of the exploration.

Typically, in patriarchal systems the masculine represents the aspect of the human psyche whose focus is outer-directed. Fueled by urges to subdue all outward forms and forces, the "he" part of us seeks dominion over the external world.

In contrast, those same male-oriented systems represent the feminine part of the human psyche as focused on the inner nature and forces. Inwardly directed, the "she" part of us is fueled by urges to surrender itself and to serve that which would gain dominion over the external world

It can't escape notice that the patriarchal-oriented systems either claim the inner Supreme as masculine or make the Supreme as external and masculine. That topic, however, is another book. This concept is only to add to our understanding and is intended to take away neither the message nor the power of the story for each of us, male or female, even though we live in a patriarchal culture.

With this focus on mastery of self in the external world, the Three Little Pigs fable lends itself to our understanding of how we are guided to excellence and mastery in the external world.

We do not stop here, however. We need to ask, "The fable is in service of what?" If we inspect gender more closely, we will see that the little male pigs are sent on their journeys by their mother – the feminine aspects of their psyches. Charged to go outward and seek their fortunes, the developmental task is done at the behest and fulfillment of their inner selves.

MOTHER PIG

Mother Pig symbolizes the unconscious nurturing source, the psyche, the collective memory of culture, the Universal Mother. A pig's entire view of life is fed to the young pigs through her. Living with mother – a loving power, but the *only* power – is having everything magically taken care of. Though they do not know it, she is the three pigs' own selves, the giver of all life. From her appears all that is needed without any effort on the part of the little pigs. Mother Pig embodies ego and culture, showing her children how to live their lives, telling them what must be remembered, defining their roles, shaping their beliefs, preserving essential stories and music and dance.

Each pig's connection with this major source is immature and mostly unconscious. Their connection does not have the power of an awakened relationship and remains, therefore, naïve. In order to make the connection to their source real and potent, the pigs must become aware of, build upon, and go beyond their ties to their mother.

2

TALE OF THE WOLF

IN THE EVENINGS *after the pigs had eaten supper, Mother Pig would clean up the kitchen and ready the children for bed.* ❦ *Dressed in pajamas, the little pigs would eagerly gather around their mother in front of the hearth.* ❦ *Then she would tell them stories – stories of queens and kings, stories of great acts and small, stories of caution and warnings, and stories of the big bad wolf who lived in the nearby forest.* ❦ *Those stories often made their little curly tails straighten in fear.* ❦ *Each night she ended her fable with an instruction to be wary of the big bad wolf because he was fond of eating little pigs.*

THE WOLF IN THIS TALE is the darkness, the feared one. He is the designated evil one or the exalted excellent one. Both evil and exaltation are feared and rejected by many individually and culturally. The wolf represents each pig's dark side, the shadow, the individual and collective unacceptable aspects of the pig's psyche. The wolf is actually created by mother pig's fears and the pigs' naïveté. What culture and the pigs cannot and do not claim in themselves becomes the presence, fiber, and behavior of the wolf.

Culture and ego each form wolves for us by compelling us to develop certain sides of ourselves and deny others. They say to us: "Be a good boy," "Girls don't do that," "Never tell a lie," "Girls are pretty and nice," "Boys don't cry," "Don't touch yourself there," "Do what you are told."

Without judging whether any of these edicts are correct, we see they stand as imperatives to encourage and condone the hard, physical, aggressive, intellectual masculine mythology as the exclusive formula of success for men, while discouraging or despising the development of the soft, sensitive, surrendering, intuitive models of mythology as the formula of abandonment for men. Conversely it encourages and condones the soft, sensitive, surrendering, intuitive feminine mythology as the exclusive formula of success for women and discourages features of the hard, physical, aggressive, intellectual feminine mythology as the formula of abandonment for women. This encouragement and discouragement leaves men and women in denial of their "whole" and their ultimately greater story.

Our greatness is often fearfully shoved aside by comments like, "I could never do that," "Girls aren't good at math," "Wow, you are a genius!" or "Only they can do such great things."

This conscious denial, at times essential for our individual and collective preservation, leaves much of what is feared, unheard, and unseen to develop in the darkness of our unconscious mind. All that culture considers good, it relegates to the light of awareness, and all that it considers bad, it ignores and relegates to the darkness of ignorance. Both are endorsed in the name of the protective community. The womb of darkness holding our forgotten pasts – along with our unknown futures – is then maligned by culture and the ego because our despised selves and our evils are buried there. Culture and ego both blame the darkness for what they hide in it.

It is also true that some feared drives and behaviors are appropriately suppressed. To have a fencing-off and constraining process protects the social and psychological containers in which we live. Yet, much of what comes to be repressed will eventually rob us of access to what will become necessary and useful threads in the fabric of our developing selves.

Until then we form our own wolf out of this incomplete fabric. We do this by ignoring or repressing everything we do not want to see or know. In reality, the wolf is our unacceptable instincts, perfection, fears, anger, violence, insecurity, power, sexuality, excellence, and so on buried in our innate darkness. There we hide away thoughts of divinity, revenge, jealousy, freedom, socially inappropriate animal behaviors, unity, surrender, incest, rage, greed, physical abuse. In our own darkness our fears go bump in the night and in that experience "I scare me with myself."

An example of repressing unacceptable behavior can be seen in a woman who often complained about a quality she despised in other women. She found weakness in women to be distasteful, manipulative, and annoying. Whenever she judged women to be less strong than herself, she saw weakness. Her reaction to this quality was to refuse to take on a "weak" stance herself and to compulsively challenge any woman she encountered using it. By making these women the designated evil ones, she then did not have to look at her own weakness. She was blind to her own manipulative behavior. The "despised" persons were reflections of her own need to render life harmless, and the wolf she created was formidable indeed.

PROJECTION

Projection is attributing our own arousal to others. It is locating our own experience outside of our self unto "the other." This relocation has the quality of giving what we have placed on "the other" the character of accurately identifying "them."

Having the capability of alienating our magnificence, our fears, our despised self, we acquire a way of coping with the parts of our self not socially or personally permitted or validated moment-to-moment in our life. In so doing, we use projection as a means of navigating our psychological and social environment. We can now carry with us what we have learned about what is not acceptable and make sure it does not appear as part of our character.

Thus liberated from the affliction, we live untouched, no longer responsible for possessing the magnificent or the despised characteristic. We rest secure, reading our intentions and experiences into the behavior of others and exalt or despise them for it.

What has been repressed and hidden in the darkness becomes unavailable for scrutiny and "choiceful" use. The question to ask is, "How might we make what is hidden available again for learning and growth as we mature?" Projection is one answer.

There is good news and bad news about projection for learning. The woman in the story above projected her despised, evil self onto "weak" women. The good news is that as a core human learning strategy, projection allowed the woman to use other women to parade her disowned self before her outwardly turned eyes. Her own invisible disowned self as a projected face worn by " the other" gave her the opportunity to observe, reflect, learn, claim, and absorb a larger, previously invisible self. This woman, however, chose to live with the bad news of projection; the refusal to learn. By denying any kinship with "weakness" her self-righteous purity continuously robbed her of the opportunity to carefully prospect and mine her feared despised self for the gold of self-knowledge. Through her projection she emptied herself of entire domains of action because she refused to examine them. Over time, the vacancy left her hollow and incomplete.

"From these repressed qualities, which are not admitted or accepted because they are incompatible with those chosen, the shadow is built up"[1] When this shadow is not accepted or explored, it functions outside of our awareness and our lack of scrutiny gives it added power.

The darkness also holds the collective denials of culture that it projects onto groups, defining them as evil in some way. Because it has displaced its unacceptable drives onto this "outside" group, society can feel both pure and safe. Criminals, for example, hold our collective acts of violence. Blacks embody our fear of darkness while indigenous Americans hold the shame and guilt of genocide in the Americas. Homosexuals hold our cultural rejection of same-sex admiration and women hold the anxiety of annihilation by the creative force. These groups are our fears projected as our despised selves. They carry our evil, relieving us of the burden. We are not evil; they are. The pigs are innocent; the wolf is bad.

The big bad wolf at this juncture is created by mother pig. He may be put away to live deep in the dark woods, but he is very much present and has a significant influence on the three little pigs.

3
DEPARTURE

ONE DAY *while watching her children at play, the wise mother pig knew that at last it was time for her children to go out on their own to seek their fortunes.* ❧ *So with tears in her eyes and final words of caution about the wolf, she sent them off, each on his separate way, to face the world.*

THE THREE LITTLE PIGS are about to embark on a new venture. Until now they have lived only one side of life – the side of innocence and light. Now they must enter into a world where both sides of life – light and darkness – co-exist. The pigs' departure will bring them into contact with the unknown, into contact with the darkness they have ignored and been taught to despise. As we have seen, much of their self-definition and personal power was acquired from their mother; they ceded the rest to those forces that function in the darkness outside of their awareness.

On their quest the pigs must now encounter what has been rendered unacceptable and invisible by culture and their own development through mother pig's stories. They must become aware of the paradox of life, that which Nicholas of Cusa calls the "coexistence of opposites."[2] The pigs' departure will now take them into the real world. The wolf lives there too.

Joseph Campbell says that departure is an essential step on the hero's quest[3] and one which is found in the mythology of all cultures. East Indian Nachiketa departs from home to eventually confront the God of Death, Australian Aborigines go " walk about," American Indians embark on a vision quest. Judaism's bar mitzvah, Catholicism's sacrament of Confirmation, society's "coming out" parties and marriages also serve as significant symbols of departure. The motif of departure in fables often includes being sent off by a parent figure of the opposite sex. The miller's daughter is sent on her encounter with Rumplestilskin because of her father's bragging; Jack begins his adventure on the beanstalk after being sent to market by his mother; Beauty is sent to the beast by her feckless father; Hiawatha's quest is inspired by the stories of Grandmother Nikomia; Eve, with her eyes just opened, is ordered from the garden into the world by her Heavenly Father.

Embarking on a new venture is at once a delicate as well as a powerful occurrence. As we depart from the safety of the known, we enter the mystery of life's unknowns. The change signals that our ensuing approach to the world will be quite different from the way it was before.

INITIATION

Psychological and spiritual maturing at each stage of development depends upon our readiness. We must always step outside the protection of the Garden of Eden to be initiated into maturity. What we do with what we encounter outside the garden determines the level of initiation we will receive.

While any act that takes us across a boundary can be an initiation, self-unfoldment follows two initiatory paths: gateway initiations and process initiations. The extraordinary events of gateway initiations cause immediate change that must be assimilated over time. Process initiations, on the other hand, bring about transformation using the actions of everyday life to be enfolded into the moment.

The pigs' departure from their mother amounts to a gateway initiation, as was our first day of kindergarten or moving into our first apartment. Each brought about an abrupt change. Process initiations, however, will unfold for the pigs over time as they interact with the wolf, much as we mature over time in child rearing while parenting.

In order to achieve a fully mature self, the pigs' shadow dimension must, for the most part, be discovered, explored, and integrated. Their maturity will evolve with the integration of the opposites of good and evil, light and dark, mother pig and wolf, self and other. This integration brings about opportunities for a maturity that would be impossible with one-sided development, whether that side be the knowledge of light or the mystery of darkness.

Integration sometimes necessitates conflict. By being faithful to what we have already learned and then encountering what is new and often contradictory, we will experience the conflict between them. Leaving home proves to be a series of conflicts between light and dark, safety and danger, known and unknown. The little pigs, for example, will be in conflict because they are going into the realm of life where the wolf lives, and they were told by their mother to avoid contact with him. In fact, contrary to what she says, contact with the wolf will become essential for the pigs' eventual integration.

Antagonistic Cooperation

In initiation, opposite forces work together to serve full self-integration. Heinrich Zimmer refers to this work as "antagonistic cooperation" stating that "every lack of integration in the human sphere simply asks for the appearance, somewhere in space and time, of the missing opposite."[4] In this way, the wolf is called forth to fill that void.

Because the pigs are naïve, they unwittingly create the wolf as despised. Because they are naïve, the wolf takes the place of the side of themselves they reject. For eventual self-mastery, however, the wolf self must be embraced. The wolf is the dark part of each pig's self, and at the same time, he is the gatekeeper at the garden of self-knowledge. In order to gain entrance, the pigs must inevitably pass by the wolf, which insists that they be impeccable before progressing to the next stages of their development. The wolf stands between the pigs and life, first as a devouring guard, next as a worthy adversary and mentor, and finally as a Merlin, Hag, or guru. He can be viewed in many roles as we develop, but he always demands to be recognized!

Lucifer and Prometheus, both dark figures, hold intriguing similarities. Lucifer's name means "light bearer," and Prometheus is the one who brought fire to humanity. Both were punished by their culture's Supreme Ruler, yet both provided invaluable contributions to humankind. A Kabbalist rabbi friend once gave me an enlightening interpretation of Lucifer that confirmed these similarities. According to esoteric Jewish tradition, God chose Lucifer to tutor humanity for its eventual rule of heaven. He was the only servant wise enough and devoted enough to adhere strictly to the stewardship of knowledge. Playing the wolf for humanity, Lucifer's demand of genuine competence and wisdom from the children of God prepared and illumined them by strict trial so they could wisely rule heaven.

Another wolf is our culture's popular nemesis, Murphy. His task is the same: to demand excellence. Murphy's First Law states "If something can go wrong, it will."[5] If we attempt a change before we are capable of managing it, Murphy's Law will stop us. On one side, Murphy personifies our lack of impeccability; on the other side, Murphy ensures that we not move on until we have the competency to fully embrace the growth experience. Because our mistakes point directly to the work we need to do on ourselves in ascending to knowledge, the opportunity to correct them is Murphy's gift to us.

Life and the wolf are intertwined. Because the pigs fear mother pig's strict messages about the darkness and what lies buried in it, they associate the wolf with annihilation. When the pigs' logic is the logic of fear, the wolf becomes a source of annihilation and needs to be avoided. When the pigs' logic is the logic of engagement, the wolf becomes a source of growth and needs to be encountered. Contact with the wolf is thus paradoxical: on the one hand he is dangerous and on the other hand essential.

The wolf actually exists for the pigs' learning. Maturity, potency, and command of inner conflict occur through day-to-day contact with the wolf. In the eternal play of opposites, the wolf is the teacher, but he appears so only after the pig develops into a qualified student. Until then, the wolf remains that which devours naïve ones. Like us, the pigs will have to discover a way to live safely in the world with the wolf. Eventually, we all need to learn that the wolf can be neither tamed nor destroyed; it must be engaged.

HOUSES

The houses the little pigs live in represent what we live in as ourselves – our ego. They also represent the mask we put on to face the world – our personality. Our ego is the boundary of meaning and protection that we put around our "being-ness" and call it ourselves. As Carl Jung states, ego is, "the complex factor to which all conscious content are related. It forms its self as the center of the field of awareness…. When sensation passes through the gate of sense perception all perceptions are related to a central theme."[6]

Relating all inputs of the senses to a central theme is the mode of operation of the ego. This central theme is what we call "me." We are housed in those themes. They give us protection and stand as our personal meaning.

Each of the little pigs is housed in his own meaning and experiences. It is no surprise that each successive man encountered gives the respective little pig building materials for his house without requiring any exchange. In each case the materials – straw, sticks, and bricks – plus all they symbolize are qualities that already belong to the pigs. The materials are resources inherited through their mother. From parental symbiosis to hoped-for wisdom of old age, each pig possesses the raw potential to continually expand or build anew the lodging of his awareness.

4

THE HOUSE OF STRAW

T HE FIRST LITTLE PIG *waved good-bye to his mother and dashed away, skipping gaily down the road.* ❨ *By and by he came upon a man carrying a load of straw.* ❨ *"Mr. Man," he said, "will you please give me some straw to build my house?"* ❨ *The man gave him all he wanted and the little pig set to building his house of straw.* ❨ *He hurried with construction and was soon dancing and playing in the sun again.*

THE STRAW USED by the first little pig to build his house can be viewed as a base potential made into a useable structure. In itself, potential is impotent until made actual, and therefore potent through awareness, use and integration.

In his naïveté the first little pig knows only how to be aware of what is temporary and flimsy. Because his awareness is limited and unsophisticated, flimsy substances are all he can request. He can build only with what he has already claimed as his own substance; his house is the symbol of himself. We may even say that the little pig builds his new life with straw.

Although a coarse, base substance, the grossest of the grasses, straw proves insubstantial to stand up to the intensities of life. The flimsiness of straw corresponds to the first pig's whimsical nature. He is a child – naïve, mostly unconscious, easily impressionable, and ignorant of his connection to life. The little pig acts just like a wide-eyed farm boy coming to the big city for the first time. A huckster's delight. His innocence makes him an easy victim and vulnerable prey for the wolf.

First Pig Thinkers

First pig thinkers are adults who have not significantly matured their worldview beyond what they were given in childhood. They naïvely still think and do as they were told by mother pig with mostly no investment of their own reflection. Believing what they have inherited to be right and good, first pig adults prefer to live a life solely within the patterns handed down by mother pig.

All of us do some first pig thinking. The first pig part of us is naïve and innocent. In a child, this innocence charms and evokes protection from those more powerful. In an adult, however, that same naïveté and innocence can become tedious, at times evoking abuse. Imprisoned at this childhood stage of ego development, life for an adult is superficial even though it is thought to be full by the first pig thinker.

First pigs, like children, do not yet own themselves. Similar to children, first pig adults are easily trespassed by the will of others. Comparable to a magnet, they can draw abusive people to themselves.

First pig adults often establish brittle, rigid boundaries as their defense against a world that is seen as threatening to blow through their flimsy barriers. This weak fortification at times gives the appearance of strength, but actually it is a frail facade covering an insubstantial vulnerability.

If this lack of maturity is sustained as the exclusive source of making sense for life, the adult first pig has the defense strategies of a child with an equal lack of sophistication and control.

One first pig thinker, a naïve and retiring woman, avoided serious or in-depth conversations with men. As a child she was taught to do whatever men told her. Her weak boundaries left her unprotected and compelled her to obey once a man made any advance in her direction. Even though she had the status of a medical doctor, in her first pig defense against life, she kept all her encounters with men light, frivolous, and superficial. She never allowed men close enough to obligate her or make her a victim of their cultural "authority." Consequently, in adult life where she now had power over her own acts, her needs were left unmet and her opinions were rarely, if ever, expressed. She was still making sense of life with the disempowered strategy of her immature, first pig self. She wanted to be safe which required her needs and wants to be magically fulfilled and understood because she couldn't risk making them known. The tragedy of this behavior left her alone, locking out satisfying adult relationships, and thoroughly hiding her wolf.

Unexamined Assumptions

All of us are first pigs to some extent. From the first pig position we will find that many of our assumptions about life have gone unexamined. First pig thinkers use this unexamined form as their primary method of engagement and meaning- making. First pig thinkers, all of us to varying degrees, cling to these assumptions although they no longer serve us as well as they did when the behaviors were the best we could do. This part of us has no understanding of why we believe as we do. We just believe that way.

From this inherited position, we do not know how to defend a belief that we have yet to understand. So embedded is our first pig self in its inherited view of reality that when the view is challenged we feel threatened.

It is possible to know when the first pig part of us has been provoked because we abruptly escalate our encounters with others to anger or even rage. We defend our position with hostility that is barren of logic or that has no substance behind it. This is often difficult for others to live with. Our first pig, self-professed rightness and goodness, generally causes others to experience us as self-righteous.

If we do not periodically re-examine what we are given by our mother pig, we run the risk of exclusively using this unexamined form of thinking all of our life.

FIRST PIG VULNERABILITIES

A large part of our selfhood is established at the first pig stage of our development in childhood. Rather than ripening these dimensions of our ego into an adult self, we often "lock in" childhood forms of deflective behaviors. These naïve deflections then end up defining us.

Defining behaviors are originally practiced by our less-than-mature self to insure its survival. As a result of our lack of maturity, however, we are left with able parts of our self-hood hardy able to function on our behalf as a strong ego. Instead, these behaviors are etched in stone from an immature, disempowered stance leaving us equipped with low substance and armed with bluster in the face of insurmountable peer, adult, or cultural forces.

All of us have many of these behaviors within us. There are adults who do not mature beyond the bulk of these unexamined assumptions, and remain stranded with it as their dominant stance in life. Their ego is not their own. It remains underdeveloped and flimsy like the straw house.

First pig thinkers can establish brittle, rigid boundaries as a defense against a world that has historically invaded their flimsy barrier. This rigidity gives them the appearance of strength, but it is actually a facade covering a childish, vulnerable, weak, and often frightened self. First pigs can put on a menacing face or behavior to all they encounter lest anyone gets a peek into their inadequacy. Their fear is that any contact might become a trespass to destroy the vulnerable underdeveloped ego that is being shielded with a ferocious demeanor.

I remember a colleague with whom I attended a seminar. During the seminar we struck up an easy friendship and became partners in acting out a family scenario as part of the seminar training. In the role play, I found her actions to be unnecessarily uncooperative, and at times vicious. I then became cool and distant toward her. During the group debriefing session, she publicly asked me what had changed during our role playing. As we dialoged, I discovered that whenever she was in the child's role she felt vulnerability that for various reasons was still very present for her today. As she acted, she experienced all parent-like power figures as threats and immediately used *all* of her resources to keep them away. After our dialog, her fear and quick ferocity deepened my understanding of, and compassion for, first pig adults.

Let us return to our story to see how the first pig fared.

5

STRAW GOES DOWN

AFTER A SHORT TIME, *who should appear on the road but the big, bad wolf.* ❦ *Seeing the little pig, he began to drool, and without a thought, as if impelled, he rushed forward to eat the little pig up.* ❦ *The pig scurried into his house of straw squealing with terror, just managing to slam the door in the wolf's face.* ❦ *Very angry, the Wolf growled, "Little pig, little pig, let me come in!"* ❦ *The pig feebly replied, "No, no no! Not by the hair of my chinny, chin, chin!"* ❦ *"Well then," said the wolf mockingly, "I'll huff, and I'll puff, and I'll blow your house in."* ❦ *So the wolf inhaled deeply, his massive chest expanding like a bellows, and he huffed and he puffed and he easily blew the house in.* ❦ *In a flash, he then greedily ate up the little pig, squeal and all.*

So much for naïveté! Ignorance of the darkness is no match for its power. The little pig thought he was ready for life, but he was aware of only a very narrow range of resources. His naïve, compensating behavior shut down possibilities for important future human interactions that would have provided experiences and resources necessary for later stages of development.

By not analyzing and digesting the stories he swallowed whole at his mother's knee, he came to live an unexamined life. The strength he possessed was not his strength; the right answers he professed were not his answers. The resulting lack of protection and self-knowledge did not prepare him for life's intensity. He knew how to be protected and taken care of, but he did not know how to protect and take care of himself. Like his house, the structure of his ego was very weak and made him incapable of standing up to life. Ignorance made him vulnerable and through it, life consumed him.

In fairy tales, the motif of purity through innocence is a common theme. Instances of purity defined as youth and freedom from worldly knowledge typically win command of the realm. In this fairy tale motif the requirement proves to be different. Command of the realm demands purity acquired through maturity. The philosopher-theologian, Thomas Aquinas, remarked that "purity is the ability to see things as they really are."[7]

Personal development occurs in stages. We learn how to be appropriately competent on one level of development before moving on to the next. The first level serves as a foundation for the second level, the second for the third, and so on.

As we have seen, the first pig stage corresponds to childhood and the beginner's level of development. It is that part of us that knows only how to recognize and sustain what mother pig has told us. We seek to reduce everything to the simple, uncomplicated contact with the reality we have understood mother pig to tell us. We head toward the caution of Socrates, namely, "The unexamined life is not worth living."[8]

The first pig, satisfied with what is already within his awareness, frivolously has not learned anything new. Believing his strength is at its peak, he thinks he knows it all. Intellectually lazy, he acts on the first information he has received from mother pig and knowingly or unknowingly refuses to look any further. This ignorance makes him culpable and binds him inside limited thinking.

First pig thinkers also refuse to change, to examine, or to think for themselves. They refuse the route of self-inquiry, and resist chewing the solid food of life because the pre-digested mother's milk of unexamined assumptions is always there.

First pig thinking narcissistically centers on the first pig. It drives his actions. He does not notice the impact his behavior has on the larger environment. He doggedly and insensitively refers primarily, if not solely, to himself.

First pig thinking is focusing on "me" and "mine" and is not aware of "us."

It is refusing to be influenced, even when others tell us we are being hurtful.

It is selling our virgin forests for short-term profit.

It is sending jobs abroad to reduce costs, and leadership not taking the responsibility for high cost occurring in the first place.

It is insisting that our belief is the only one, ignoring a larger world's right to different beliefs.

It is stubbornly believing that where we are now is the only truth.

We may say that first pig thinking is seductive; it can be used as an excuse to avoid change. Because first pig thinkers live blithely inside their unexamined notions, they can feel good – justified and righteous – while ignoring the wider implications and outgrowth of a "good" life.

"Good" people are consumed by their wolves all the time and don't even know they are being consumed. Some of us first pigs even make a virtue out of being devoured by the wolf.

Archie Bunker, in Rob Reiner's television sitcom *All In The Family,* made a virtue out of his demand that the world be like him. But his complaining and narrowness consumed him through the loss of respect of those he loved the most.

He put his hand on his gun again, approached me, and announced that he was looking for a 6 foot, 175 pound black man. (I am a 6 foot 2 inch, 220 pound black man.) I replied that I understood the difficulty of his position (I have taught diversity training to Twin Cities law enforcement officers) but his contention that all black men looked alike caused me to feel unsafe and misrepresented by him.

The policeman replied, "That's too bad," and left the building.

I found my partner, and we prepared to leave together. But by this time we had attracted an audience in the quiet of the library. Two patrons and the librarian witnessed the interaction and came over to offer their concern about the officer's behavior. One person, a young, white, male college student, volunteered that the police were looking for a black man with a goatee. (I wear only a mustache.) He told us he had been in the library preparing an article on racism for his school newspaper. "I've never seen everyday racism before," he said excitedly, "and here it was, right in front of my eyes!"

While we were all talking, the police officer came back inside. He walked up to our group, and demanded to know if the librarian knew me. "Yes," she said, "he's a customer."

"Then what's his name?"

"I don't know," replied the flustered librarian. "We have so many …"

My partner was upset, and restated my name. The officer said, "There's a black man out there who wants to kill a cop." He added that I was "eyeballin' him."

I reiterated something to the effect that his continued pursuit of me even though I did not fit the suspect's description left me upset and unsettled. I said I was a law-abiding citizen who now felt unsafe.

"Have a nice day," he said sarcastically, and turned his back.

My partner was disturbed and later said to me in private that she thought the reverse was true. "There was a cop who wanted to kill a black man."

As I think about what happened, I realize my pain is in the law enforcement officer's inability to see me. He looks, but I am invisible to him. He sees instead a stereotype of his own making. He does not allow me to liberate myself from his damaged, frozen, and negative image. No matter what I do, I remain a perpetual suspect of crime. I am frightened that underneath the stereotype may be what my partner deduced, the fear I share with almost all black men, his desire to shoot a black man, and beneath that desire may be the "black man" who is his own self. The self that he fears, loathes, and places outside himself onto the embattled group of black men who carry the image and blame for this fear he has of himself. A line from *Blowin' In The Wind* comes to mind. "How many roads must a man walk down, before they call him a man?" What do I have to do to be able to relax, to enjoy the privilege of unencumbered citizenship? And the refrain answers me, "The answer my friend is blowin' in the wind …"

With his hand still on his weapon, the officer left. I stood there stunned. Those who had joined me, and the on-lookers who had kept their distance, were wide-eyed and disturbed. I drove home carefully, on side streets and well under the speed limit to my home on Summit Avenue. The officer rejoined the search justified that he was doing a good job. The young white male went home to finish writing a story on racism for his school paper.

First pig thinkers often do not realize the impact they have on others. That is a predicament.

An incident I witnessed will illustrate this point. On Christmas day in 1990, a twenty-three-year-old man had what he thought was a good idea. He was "inspired" to give the family dog to a troubled boy in need of a pet. So without consulting anyone in his family, the young man put a bow on the dog's collar and brought it to its new home. The probable pain to his brother and sister didn't occur to him, nor did the awful possibility of having to take the gift back. All he could see was the immediate idea of the boy needing something to love. When the repercussions of horror ripped through his family, he could not understand what all the fuss was about. He had a good idea and he did it!

THE TYRANNY OF WEAKNESS

The flimsiness of the first pig thinker's boundaries can unsettle others; this weakness can be a tyranny. When in groups, people tend to adjust their behavior to the feeblest member, while the vital feelings and behaviors of the other members often go unexpressed. For example, another man grew up in a family tyrannized by a "weak" father. No one could express excitement or voice a disagreement because they might upset father and cause him to have a heart attack.

Many people walk around on eggshells when they are manipulated by someone else's expressed or implied inability to cope with truth. This unstable ego structure characterizes adults stuck in first pig behavior: manipulative, self-centered, often tyrannical.

Mired in this narrowness, first pig thinkers are often not able or willing to be aware of others. This selfishness, somewhat acceptable in a child, proves oppressive in an adult. First pig thinkers are at times devoured by the wolf they create because they unfortunately exclude themselves from life by putting others in the position of deciding what truths, and therefore what parts of life, they can bear. Along with that tragedy, those close to the weak tyrant may create a habit of withholding sides of themselves deemed too intense. Partners and family of a first pig thinker can then become compulsive withholders, eventually withholding even from themselves.

Not surprisingly, the exclusiveness of self-indulgent weakness causes the first pig's downfall. Focus on "me" has value, but breaks down quickly when it is the only choice used, symbolized by the wolf blowing down the house of straw and eating the pig in all cases.

EXPANDING AWARENESS

How many times have we all come to a gateway in our lives only to be eaten by the wolf? We find ourselves frustrated and discouraged, cycling again and again to the same impasse and predictably being devoured. Can we ever progress beyond first pig thinking and our ideas of straw? Yes, we can, because our awareness grows with time.

Years ago, my family took a vacation to Banff National Forest in Canada. Hiking up a mountain path, we spotted wild raspberries growing in the underbrush. My nine-year-old son could not see them. Although we all pointed the berries out to him, we were amazed that he still could not spot them at all. All the way up the mountain, we picked berries to share with him, joking that we would refuse to feed him on the way down. In frustration, my son foraged carefully in the bushes until he learned to spot the raspberries for himself. Through mouthfuls of berries, he voiced his surprise that he actually had been missing them. On the way down, the rest of us, relieved of our obligation to pick berries for him, suddenly discovered strawberries growing along the path exactly where we had been picking raspberries on the way up. Why hadn't we seen them before? We realized that we shared the same lack of awareness as my son. Now, with our expanded awareness, we could all enjoy strawberries as well as raspberries, except for my son, of course, who couldn't see the strawberries at all!

In life, each of us can only see what we know how to see. Everything is always right in front of us, but our experience occurs inside our awareness. For all of us, awareness grows with time. Life manifests itself as change and growth with the rich varieties of experience present inside the same event but is locked away by our own narrowness. This is quite evident when we notice how a mature adult and a child see the same situation. As physicist Warner Heisenberg says, "We do not experience nature, but nature exposed to our method of inquiry."[10]

Let's return to our story and see what the second little pig does with the same situation.

6

The House of Sticks

THE SECOND PIG *left his mother determined to follow her advice and do well.* ❦ *Walking cautiously down the road, he came upon a man carrying a large bundle of sticks.* ❦ *The little pig said to the man, "Mr. Man, will you please give me some sticks to build my house?"* ❦ *The man gave him all he wanted and the little pig set to building his house of sticks.* ❦ *Construction took longer than it took his brother, but after careful work, the house of sticks was completed.* ❦ *Feeling he had done the right thing, he ran outside to play.*

MORE MATURE THAN HIS BROTHER, the second pig attempts to make a stronger structure to defend himself. Although conscious that this is something he needs to do, he does not know how to know what to do. Like his brother, he builds his house. Only this time he builds with the improved, yet still limited, resources he has available. He builds with sticks, a logical extension of straw. The little pig recognizes how different sticks are from straw, but he cannot realize how much they are the same.

The second little pig is trying to improve. He tries to do the right thing. He wants to please others and seeks appropriate behavior to that end. His inadequate ideas about life, however, render him confused, tentative and rigid.

Sometimes whole communities, and even entire cultures, can be second pigs. The civil rights movement of the '60's is a good instance.

The racial conflict of those years erupted from America's many decades of deep-rooted pain and tension between the economically and politically dominant white culture and the excluded and oppressed black culture. Demand for participation in "the American dream" on the one hand, and the revival of human dignity on the other, was a mobilizing theme.

Members of various racial and ethnic groups joined the black movement's leadership as they sought to make amends for long-standing inequities. In this important cultural struggle there then came a point of conflict among the leadership. Some of the black leaders took issue with the direction the movement was taking and strongly stated that the movement needed to be led by blacks only.

Movement leadership, however, was shared by members of the white culture determined to right the wrongs of the past. They showed widespread confusion at the resistance of black leadership to their acts of atonement and generosity. They were completely befuddled by the anger leveled at them by their black colleagues and felt hurt that their offers were being refused. In reflex, their hurt turned to anger.

We can say that some of the white members of the movement's leadership were trapped in second pig thinking. They did not even know how to know what they did wrong. When they did not support the idea of black leadership, they did more of the same thinking that had created the problem in the first place.

While trying to do the right thing and correct the earlier injustice, they were unaware that they were using the same thinking that had caused and perpetuated blacks' inequities. It did not occur to them to collaborate or follow the blacks. They wanted to lead the movement instead of serve the movement. That profound idea of service needed to occur spiritually as well as politically and economically.

So instead of inviting the wounded parties to plan the menu, they unwittingly offered the traditional bone of appeasement. Because the majority culture had made both decisions – oppression and freedom – on its own, its act of atonement was only an extension of the same exclusive thinking that had created the schism. They knew that exclusion and appeasement were different; they did not see that both were acts of arrogance.

THE SECOND PIG AND THE HOUSE OF STICKS

The method of the first pig was one-step thinking; the method of the second pig is one-route thinking. Without choice, the second pig binds himself by the linear sequence of events that went before. He has not yet matured to the point where he can see larger connections. Extending the norm is his only strategy for change.

This inadequate problem solving has the effect of rearranging the furniture when an entirely new structure is needed. Needless to say, the second pig was doomed to fail. He forgot the old French proverb, "The more things change, the more they remain the same."

In the period immediately following a divorce, people often use this method of extending the norm. They almost invariably find a new mate who actually embodies the same characteristics as their previous mate. The new relationship will bring up the same conflicts, or will soon show clear signs of being fitted into the mold of past unexamined behavior because, in fact, both parties bring their wolves with them.

SECOND PIG THINKING

Second pig thinking is trying to do the right thing by employing the same principles and behaviors which have repeatedly proven themselves inadequate. Taking a logical next step out of a set of beliefs that can no longer yield satisfactory results is confusing and frustrating for a second pig.

We can see this pattern in a woman who spent several years trying to heal a painful relationship with her husband. She used the "right answers" supplied by culture. Although she had already outgrown the boundaries set for women by society, she was unaware of it. Thus she could only keep trying the same remedy again and again. When he was stoic she attempted to guess what her husband was thinking. In order to please him she tried to change her character, her behavior, the environment they shared. The woman turned herself inside out trying to understand why her efforts of harmony and communication were not working. Confused and frustrated, she kept hurling herself into one improvement after another, trying to "better" herself inside the embedded expectations created for her inside culture's traditional norms for marriage. It didn't occur to her that this realm of inquiry was itself the problem. Her method of inquiry could only yield the same dysfunctional results she had found so disastrous to her relationship up until now.

This woman resembles the second pig in her use of "more of the same" as a strategy for transformation. The second pig built upon the past experience of the first pig and came up with a sound, logical answer to the problem of the wolf: use stronger vegetation. Dealing with the wolf, however, and building with sticks – an extension of straw – proved to be nothing but an extension of the same frivolous thinking.

There was once a man who circled from his therapist, to his support group, to his spiritual director, and back again to his therapist seeking advice. He ran around trying to do the right things, some of which did not feel "right" at all. He was unable to see that he had outgrown some of his values, and because of this, life became difficult for him to follow. Attempting to fit his profoundly maturing life inside of a now inadequate value system, he became frustrated and depressed. Since he used old guides for his behavior, he found himself frequently traveling down the same dead ends. Similar to the second pig's struggle, the man's struggle involved the awareness that values, like ideas, have careers, and upon periodic examination, some values will naturally be retired for more mature ones. When he was finally able to realize this, his confusion receded.

TAKING RESPONSIBILITY

Another aspect of second pig thinking is the notion that circumstances control one's life. This makes life for second pig thinkers rather ambiguous. They are apt to think that one thing after another happens to them, when actually they are doing the same thing over and over, creating the same results. In missing this point through repeating what no longer works, second pigs attempt to engage the wolf in ways that actually prevent their own survival.

Like the house of sticks in which they live, second pig thinkers are locked into a rigid, but weak system. They feel powerless to give direction to their own lives; things just seem to happen to them. They have a rather brittle idea about how life should be, most often having nothing to do with how it really is. They believe that if only others (the wolf) would stop doing things to them, their life would improve.

I used to be under the impression that other people were responsible for my emotions. When I was angry, I was sure that someone made me angry, and I could relate in detail how that was so. I likewise thought that people made me fall in love, made me sad, gave me hope, and so on. Of course, people contributed to all of these experiences, but did they really cause my experience? To the extent that I blamed others for my responses of joy or sorrow, love or apathy, I was eaten by the wolf. There was no way, however, that anyone could have convinced me of this fact. At some point, I became aware that I had many more choices than I realized and I gave myself permission to use them. In an "angry" encounter, I became aware that I could shout, cry, dissuade, ignore, laugh, or leave the room. I realized that I chose my emotions and that I was the major creative force in my life.

The second pig thinker is the victim who has the power to change, but lacks the resources, awareness, maturity, or courage to do so. Like the majority of us, he thinks having less power is having no power and thus stays bound to old dysfunctional patterns. The Charles Schultz comic strip, *Peanuts*, artfully portrays second pig thinking in its characterization of Charlie Brown. Charlie tries to kick a football held for him by his nemesis, Lucy. She unvaryingly jerks the football away at the last moment, causing him to crash unceremoniously to the ground. Lucy continually promises not to do it again, but she does it without fail. Every Charlie Brown has his Lucy; he creates her at every moment. Will he ever learn that she will always pull the football away whenever he tries to kick it? Until he does something different, things will always remain the same.

7

STICKS GO DOWN

At the setting of the evening sun, the big bad wolf spied the second little pig and confidently approached the house of sticks. ⟪ Seeing the wolf coming, the pig scurried inside his house, barred the door, and quaked in anticipation. ⟪ The wolf knocked heavily and in a booming voice said, "Little pig, little pig, let me come in." ⟪ "No, no, no! Not by the hair of my chinny chin chin," said the little pig shakily. ⟪ The impatient wolf threw back the reply, "Then I'll huff, and I'll puff, and I'll blow your house in." ⟪ So the wolf swelled himself up even bigger than before. ⟪ And he huffed and he puffed and he puffed and he huffed and he blew the house in. ⟪ He immediately ate up the astonished little pig, including his squeal.

THE SECOND PIG fared no better than his younger brother! His shift from straw to sticks was a vain attempt to accommodate change by merely doing more of the same.

The paraphrasing of an old saying applies here. "If you always do what you've always done, you'll always get what you've always gotten." The pig employed the logical extension of old behavior and got the same outcome: he got eaten. Whenever we, like the pig, attempt to use outmoded behavior, the wolf will eat us up, too.

CONSCIOUS INCOMPETENCE

When a major structure does not work for us anymore, the process of life (as well as our own sanity) demands that we stay at it until we discover why it fails. In that light, the failure of the second pig is an important dimension of growth. It points the way from conscious incompetence to conscious competence. The second pig showed us conscious incompetence; things did not work for him, he knew they didn't, but he did not know why. Conscious incompetence provides an essential ingredient for human and spiritual development by keeping us pressed against our developmental edge in the midst of failure until we realize why we fail. This makes failure very valuable.

Then, once we've knowingly experienced things not working, we are in the position to move on to conscious competence: understanding why things work, changing ourselves, and making efforts to keep it so.

For millennia mystics have recognized and used this natural occurrence with their students. Students are kept standing on the cutting edge of growth until they become aware of those behaviors that no longer satisfactorily serve them. The teachers ensure that they remain in this state of creative incompetence until they realize the truth.

A friend of mine, a dynamic natural leader, was consistently unable to achieve significant leadership positions when he joined groups. He would advance to the position of second best, and then at some point in the process, he would be viewed as a threat to the organization's leaders and inevitably be walled out. In his late forties he came to understand that his "incompetence" to be number one was, in some way, his own choice. Indeed, in his youth he did not behave as a leader, even though he had potential, and as he matured into competency over the years, he did not behave any differently than in his youth. He did not know how to assert his competence. The man was unaware of the depth of his habit of being second best which blocked any insight to his childhood feelings of inadequacy and shame buried deep in his shadow. With just a little effort his wolf was able to blow in his unexamined house of sticks. A wise mentor intervened, and artfully helped him work through many layers of fear. It was then that he matured to greater insight and expanded the ways he expressed himself.

To develop further, the second pig will, in some fashion, have to take charge of his experience of reality. The meaning he makes of his experience will evolve to where, in the next stage of his development, he will feel in charge of his destiny. He will eventually come to realize that his destiny has more to do with his own insight about how things work in the world than just mother pig's explanations. He will learn to defend himself against the wolf and against others in his world. He will then move to the essential next step of developing the defenses of a strong ego.

Moving beyond second pig thinking requires an expansion of contact with life; growth into mature behavior is imperative. Until then, second pig thinkers will live a life of developmental drift, unaware of what works for them, and what doesn't. Until then, life will confuse and consume them. Until then, they will be unable to engage the wolf and survive. Until then, their lack of maturity will lock out essential awareness for satisfactory contact with life. Until then, they will get eaten every time.

8

HOUSE OF BRICKS

T HE THIRD LITTLE PIG *was sad when he left home, as is often true in partings.* ❦ *Walking down the road, he met a man with a hod of bricks.* ❦ *The pig said to the man, "Mr. Man, will you please give me some bricks to build my house?"* ❦ *The man gave him all he wanted and the little pig set to building his house of bricks.* ❦ *It was a long and difficult task and he completed it with a deep sense of satisfaction.* ❦ *Then he went outside to plant his garden.*

THE SHIFT FROM BEING the victim to having defenses against victimization is the initiation symbolized by the brick house. In building it, the third pig passed through a gateway to a new beginning. He had some way to withstand the often confusing, and at times overwhelming, complexities of life represented by the assault of the wolf.

The third pig was secure and prepared for going into the world. He had pondered deeply the stories told by his mother, he understood how his world worked and out of that understanding had fashioned his safe home. Instead of the symbiosis and self-righteous arrogance of the first pig, the third pig's self-assurance developed from the thorough infusion of mother pig. Instead of being reflexively locked into the victim role and the approval seeking of the second pig, he had discovered how things work and had gotten on the good side of them. He had mastered mother pig's world. He knew how to be safe.

This position allowed him the respite to cultivate the developmental shifts that would prepare him for his future adventures with the wolf. Inner safety gave him the confidence to rely on himself and create the secure inner dwelling – a house of bricks.

As if pigs were habituated to being devoured, the first two pigs compulsively repeated their unexamined behavior and were eaten by the wolf. The brothers made decisions based on conditioning, much like someone steering a motorboat by looking back at the wake, eventually coming around into the same errors (and into the wolf's mouth) every time.

Stepping beyond the decisions of the first two pigs in a radically different fashion, the third pig made a move of genius: a house of bricks. The logical extension of straw is sticks; the logical extension of sticks is logs. But in realizing that the extension is merely more of the same thing, the third pig made a radical shift of thinking.

This reminds me of the Monty Python comedy group who, when unable to make a logical transition from one skit to the next, sent someone on stage to announce: "And now for something completely different." Like this proclamation, the third pig did something completely different from anything pigs had tried before.

We are all like the third pig because defenses are important in our development. They are necessary because they sustain us and give us a sense of security and self-esteem in the face of life's more overwhelming experiences. The third pig's initiation allowed him to make himself safe, albeit temporarily, against the wolf and others in his life who would have him live as they see fit. The brick house of defenses is critical for the pig because later in his development it will allow him continued awareness of the wolf and the ability to stay in contact with everything the wolf represents.

The third pig's sadness when he left home speaks to his promise of maturity. He was aware of the act of departure from mother pig in a way different from his brothers.

When the first pig dashed gaily away with no sense of needing a structure of safety, he found additional safety to be unnecessary. His world was already defined and structured as surely as himself. Oblivious to his lack of preparedness for a life measurably different from his fragile and rigid view, the first pig wove a flimsy structure together because it was all he felt called to do.

The second pig was cautious as he departed, determined to follow mother pig's warnings. His success was assured and his work was done because he had been so careful to make decisions with the truths he was given. He always did the right things. He would do this even when the "right things" no longer worked for him.

Our third pig had been protected at home and was also sent out on his own at mother pig's bidding. She determined that he had whatever he needed. The third pig experienced a sense of what was before him, but unlike his first pig brother, he knew there was a difference between himself and the world he was entering. Unlike his second pig brother, he set himself apart from some of the things mother pig taught them as he inherited and oversaw the realm of safety and prosperity that his mother created. He was sad, but determined to do what he had to do in order to gain the vision she gave him. To this end, the third pig built a house where he believed he would be safe.

Like developing a mature garden, the pig must now endure the realities he is given and mature in its lessons. He will become the guardian of what mother pig created. He will seek to insure that everyone stay within the constraints of what mother pig gave, just as he has done. His brick house of safety and the fruits of his garden will serve him in good stead, "until they don't."

9

THE BRICKS HOLD

Some time later, *the big bad wolf spied the little pig working outside his home.* ❰ *He walked boldly up to the gate.* ❰ *The little pig saw him coming and quickly ran into his house, bolting the door.* ❰ *The wolf was quite confident in getting what he wanted because he had been so successful with the other pigs.* ❰ *So he knocked arrogantly on the door saying, "Little pig, little pig, let me come in."* ❰ *The little pig haltingly answered, "No, no, no! Not by the hair of my chinny chin chin."* ❰ *The wolf smirked, "Right. That's what your brothers said, and I ate them up. If you don't open the door, I'll huff and I'll puff, and I'll blow your house in."* ❰ *He blew himself up so big that the buttons popped right off his shirt.* ❰ *He released a gale of wind against the door.* ❰ *He huffed and he puffed, and he*

puffed and he huffed, and he huffed and he puffed again.
❨ All to no avail. ❨ The brick house stood steady against
his assault. ❨ The astounded wolf lay spent at the door,
temporarily defeated.

At last a pig who can stand up to the wolf. The ingenuity
of his decision to try something different paid off. The assault
of the wolf was formidable, as it often is in life, but the pig
survived. He saved his squeal!

Though frightened, the third pig remained safe inside his
house. Its bricks and mortar represent the evolutionary learning of species and myth, of institutional and individual

preservation, claimed as his own. Now he can live within those walls, a sanctuary against the wolf. In another sense, moving into the brick house represents the change from adolescence to adulthood. For most of us, adult interactions provide a much more empowered (and thus safe) environment than the vulnerable stages of childhood and adolescence.

The third pig created a structure in which he sustains himself in the face of the wolf's onslaught. Because of his safety, he will have continued and sustained contact with the wolf, and as a result, a whole new dimension of learning can take place. The first two pigs could not survive with the wolf. They locked themselves out of this survival opportunity; their naïveté was their defeat.

When my daughter was an adolescent, she was intimidated by an elite clique that had formed in her school. Her feelings of intimidation interfered with her school work and her social life. So upset was she that she even threatened to quit the school. That weekend her favorite uncle came to visit. He spent considerable time with her and provided a new perspective on her worth. By Monday morning she was able to create a defense to help herself: she decided that she didn't care what the clique thought of her; she didn't need them. Thus fortified against the power wielded by the group, she was able to excel again in the larger school community.

She didn't need to reconcile herself with the clique; she merely had to reach within herself to find the resources of self-esteem – and thus social safety – already within her. Approval of a higher order fit the bill. Her status was raised by the approval of a twenty-year-old male. She no longer needed sanctioning. Later in life she would have many opportunities to re-examine the initiation that served her then.

The re-examination of powerful defensive behavior that gives one culturally-sanctioned reward is shown in the next story.

One warm summer afternoon, a group of friends spilled out onto the front porch to enjoy a whisper of breeze and tall glasses of sun tea. A disagreement started between their host and hostess and soon escalated into an argument. As if animated by an invisible force, they each became entrenched in repetitive and intractable defensive positions, their stubbornness made even more difficult by the presence of their friends.

The husband was losing ground and beginning to sound as if he was more interested in winning than in getting to the bottom of the conflict. Suddenly he turned on his heel and stomped into the house.

In the awkward hush that followed, a few weak jokes were tried to melt the tension, but they failed. Shortly, the door opened again and the husband re-emerged wearing all of his clothes inside out and backwards. When he went inside the house, he realized that his defenses were working against him, cutting off his ability to communicate. To embody his insight, he decided to dress the part.

His strange appearance at the door was so unlike his usual self that it radically changed the atmosphere on the porch. The shift brought delight to the guests and allowed the couple to resolve their difference almost instantaneously. Their usual argument historically followed an established formula of dysfunctional interaction. They had an unconscious agreement that required them to act out the whole sad script. This time the husband interrupted the pattern by doing something different. His insight and the shift in climate brought a totally new and unknown solution into existence. They could now choose. And it was completely different.

A PRISONER OF SAFETY

There is much more for the third pig to learn. This step is

only the beginning of a new level in his journey. Inside the security of himself, the third pig will eventually come to realize that what he has figured out about how things work and how to be safe is not as total and permanent as he thought.

As we mature, some of the defenses we developed against the wolf and others cease being useful. We mature to the point where we no longer need to be constantly vigilant against every trespass or threat to our ego. We grow in skill and stature. We become strong and skillful enough to be in contact with life, survive, and learn while we are doing it. We become strong enough to be vulnerable.

This insight is not for the second pig. A second pig must first develop a strong ego. He must first acquire strong defenses and master vigilance before he will even begin to question its effectiveness. The second pig is a victim. He is not strong enough yet to be vulnerable.

As for the third pig, he soon begins to realize that he has become a prisoner of his own brick house of safety.

When the third pig chose something different to build with, he likewise opened the possibility for a different outcome. For this building material he tapped the underlying source, the substance of the unconscious, symbolized by the earth and her firmness.

This shift from sticks to the substance of earth is a shift of genius. The third pig made a structure based on his knowledge of personal and cultural security. He used the knowledge of the first two levels of awareness (his brothers), and came to understand how things work. By creating something new from earth, water, and fire, the pig set the stage to consciously recreate his own experience of life. With his security readily at hand, he no longer needs to be bound by the limitations of security. He is now solidly prepared for the future dimensions of his quest: facing the wolf.

DEVELOPMENTAL READINESS

Departure from the brick house signals a monumental step in the third pig's development. All that he has gone through up to this point has prepared him for the life pilgrimage he is about to undertake. He has developed a base that provides him with a shield that he will eventually come to use as an instrument rather than a mandate. By virtue of his maturity, he is developmentally ready to be deeply influenced by life. No longer constrained by naïveté, he is equipped to respond to the call that will deepen his maturity.

His risk, however, is threefold:

1. Guarding his safety, the pig risks staying where he is. He does this by turning to what he knows how to do even though the behaviors no longer satisfy him. In this way he seeks to nourish himself with tried conventions that no longer have substance for his development. He employs acts that were necessary, made sense, and helped him grow in earlier periods of his life.

   As first pigs were locked into one step thinking and second pigs were enmeshed in one pattern thinking, so the third pig can be trapped in fixed ways of being (gestalts). These fixed ways and behaviors no longer contain the resources that can feed his innate desire to go beyond himself, nor can they respond to the future call to action with the wolf. Seeking a promotion, a new relationship, more education or training – all useful on their own merit – will eventually cease to satisfy the developmental craving to grow.

2. Counterfeiting wisdom and insight puts the third pig's maturation at risk, or at least postpones it. He counterfeits when he alters himself just enough to embezzle the image of what he thinks is next. Because of his lack of authentic-

ity, he remains embedded in his defended self and uses what he misappropriates to bury himself even deeper in his cherished, yet no longer fully relevant, safety. This inauthentic behavior, which is motivated by fear, deflects this third pig's opportunity to act on his developmental readiness.

Counterfeiting is the misappropriation of the appearance of development. It may take the form of a caring and sensitive person, by someone who does not have those virtues, in order to gain social benefits. Another counterfeiting form is someone with a superficial perusal of a field who creates the impression of having deep knowledge of the subject and offers to teach others its intricacies and scope.

3. Putting his safety at risk, the third pig ventures out of his realm of safety and competence. He does this through measured engagement with the wolf. This is the price of knowledge that promises wisdom.

If he can put aside being wed to his safety, the third pig will be on the way to learning the difference between imprisonment and security. One victory against the dark side cannot yield maturity, however. The wolf will return, as most assuredly, he must.

10

THE TURNIP PATCH

Now the wolf, *we must understand, is very wise.* ❦ *He has spent a lifetime demolishing houses and devouring the pigs inside.* ❦ *Having learned from all of those experiences, he concluded that it was useless to attempt to penetrate the third pig's fortress directly.* ❦ *So he went away to think about new tactics.* ❦ *Some time later he returned to the brick house, knocked at the door, and in a very friendly manner addressed the third pig again, "Little pig, this struggle between us is senseless.* ❦ *Come with me to Farmer Brown's turnip patch tomorrow morning.* ❦ *We will both be able to dig as many turnips as we like.* ❦ *Then we can have a feast together." ❦ The pig thought for a moment.* ❦ *Then he answered the wolf through the door, "That is a splendid idea." ❦ The wolf asked, "What time*

shall we meet?" ⦅ And the pig replied, "Six o'clock." ⦅
The wolf departed, confident that his plan to trick the pig
would unfold smoothly. ⦅ The little pig, not trusting the
wolf, went at five o'clock that morning. ⦅ When the wolf
came to collect him promptly at six, the pig laughed at the
befuddled wolf through the bolted door and said, "I went
at five this morning and dug a bunch of big, sweet turnips.
⦅ They are cooking on the hearth at this very moment." ⦅
The wolf was furious, but being experienced in the art of
tricking and eating pigs, he was confident that eventually
he would have his way.

THE PIG HAS TRICKED THE WOLF! He has taken another significant step. He's becoming smart! Not wise, mind you, but smart. The wolf has behaviors that he uses to be successful; the pig now claims some of them for himself. In order to do so, however, the third pig must have some measured contact with the wolf. He becomes his initiate, and this leads to another critical point.

SECURITY VS. IMPRISONMENT

While sheltered naïvely behind the underdeveloped truths of his defenses, the third pig presumed himself to be able to master life on his own terms. The victory of his defenses, albeit temporary, led him to believe his security made him impervious to the wiles of the wolf. Now he discovers that he must step outside his sanctuary in order to engage a deeper reality and learn from life.

There is virtually no precedent in the pig's life for what he must do: move from the safe, defended existence of the brick house into the dangerous specter of the unknown where the wolf also resides. He must take another look at his safety. Now he sits inside a sanctuary of his own making, comfortable, secure, safe, yet he is also imprisoned by his own invulnerability. He is ultimately lonely.

When I started developing the Pigs Eat Wolves model in the early 1970's, I was a consultant to a drug treatment center for adolescents. One day I directed the residents to act out the story of the three pigs. The first pig assumed that he had the resources for sobriety and didn't need to remain in treatment. In short order, the first pig was back into "using" alcohol and drugs. The second pig completed treatment, but committed two errors. First, he assumed that he didn't need the support of aftercare. Second, the second pig continued to frequent the friends and haunts of his abusive lifestyle. Gulp!

He, too, was eaten by the wolf.

The third pig represented someone who had successfully gone through a treatment program and was participating in aftercare. The wolf in this drama, of course, represented one dimension of the dark side – the desire to get "high." The wolf continually attempted to seduce the third pig to come out of his house and use alcohol and drugs. The third pig refused. In the debriefing after the drama, the young woman who played the third pig reported that it was boring in the house. She said she felt safe there, but knew that life, fun, and growth was out where the wolf was. We then moved to the important and much-needed discussion of what it would take to have a contented sobriety.

The third pig, like us, has to operate from safety in order to survive long enough to learn. If not, the same fate will befall him as befell his brothers. He will be eaten. The pig, however, will never continue to develop and discover himself in the safety of the brick house. In order to grow, we will eventually have to take risks. That risk is to face the wolf. It is through contact with others that our wolf becomes evident. We all require others in our life. Through others we see who we are. For knowing ourselves we must make ourselves available to be touched deeply, and this happens only in relationship.

By design, our defenses regulate our ability to be touched deeply or influenced in relationships. Over time, however, we come to find that in certain valued relationships we are automatically defending ourselves when it does not serve us. We may find that we are cut off from that core which fulfills our life. So adept are we at being ourselves that we put the strength of our defenses at risk of becoming our weakness. We have become so effective at being ourselves that we cannot develop any further than where we are.

Defenses vs. Reality

Walls of defense are designed to control life and render it harmless. Through his success in building defenses, the pig realized his power. There is a certain arrogance here, born out of the fresh experience of power. The pig prematurely thinks he has life all figured out. He is the architect that designed the defenses to keep the wolf out and he is the guard that protects his vulnerability against harm. Eventually the pig comes to realize that he is imprisoned inside the brick walls of his defenses and later still, he realizes that he himself is the warden as well as the prisoner.

Many of us become so strategic and successful with our defenses that we bind ourselves to narrowly constructed reality. We confuse our defenses with reality. Our defenses are not truth; they are simply what have kept us safe so far.

When, as a maturing third pig, we take the risk to venture out where the wolf is, we are ready to claim more of ourselves, and thus more of our power. At this time in our development some relationships that we have avoided, or that have been beyond our reach, are now manageable. Because of our growing strength they are now merely grist for the mill.

A woman, who had been sexually abused as a child, had built very strong defenses against men. She decided to have nothing to do with men and resolved to trust none who resembled her abusers. In order to be safe, her defenses were well advised and served her appropriately. Through great effort she grew in power. Her defenses against men eventually became awesome. As she then matured, she began to realize that important and valuable dimensions of her psyche for next steps in her maturation were not available to her. Her painful realization was that she couldn't just turn her psyche off in one instance and back on in another.

Rebounding in defensive anger, she blamed the group who hurt her for her lack of trust and absence of that dimension of friendship in her life. After some years, she became strong enough to acknowledge that she herself had built her brick house for safety and remained locked inside by the turn of her own key. Reflecting on this insight, she determined to take charge of her experience of life. Understanding that she had grown enough to be competent and strong, she thought about opening the door and venturing out beyond her retreat into herself. She didn't go out naïve, however. She knew that her defenses were a resource that she could call upon at a moment's notice. As a matter of fact, they were so effective that she knew her work was being able to hold them at bay. Now she was secure but no longer imprisoned.

PROJECTION

Like the woman above, the pig initially blames the wolf for his imprisonment, and only eventually realizes that he alone is responsible for being locked in the house. The victim is not blaming himself, but he comes to understand that he has grasped merely a part of truth. Yes, he survived by doing the best he could given the circumstances of his life. But, at this point, by acknowledging his role in creating his limitations, as did the woman in the story above, the pig put himself in charge of what to do with the rest of his life. That key insight interrupts the pattern of his victimization by interrupting his part in it. In this way, the pig lays claim to mastery within his dilemma.

As long as the third pig blames someone else for his condition, however, he will be caught in the "justness" of his position. He will disown and project all of his evil onto the convenient "mean one" who wronged him. In this way he remains blind to the fact that his defensiveness is actually a clinging to, and keeping alive of, the destructive forces acting upon him. He doggedly carries his victimizer around in his head, heart, and gut.

By acting as if "it" is out there, the correlate "in here" dangerously bumps around in the darkness as his disowned self. The disowned one "in here" becomes even more dangerous now because of the third pig's acquired power in his brick house of safety.

RESPONDING TO THE CALL TO ACTION

Life knocks repeatedly at our door before we realize that we must step beyond the brick house. This realization will bring about the next most significant step in the pig's development, the shift in his relationship with the wolf. Much like the first interruption in the pattern of his life (leaving the safety of mother's home) the third pig now interrupts the fixed patterns of culture and his own experience. He is coming to realize that "one-sided progress is exactly like knowing half a truth. It is not truth at all."[11] He does this by actively embracing paradox; in this case, danger and safety at the same time.

For the pig, paradox now becomes a practical reality. Previously he thought one side of life true and the other side false. Now he becomes aware that risk, the other side of safety, possesses the next truths necessary for his development. Sitting unmoving at one end of any polarity leaves one lonely and disempowered, as if cut off by blinders. There is no power at either of the poles without awareness, engagement, and eventual mastery of the other side also.

The pig has to claim the power of the entire continuum that the many polarities in his life will present. He does this by dialoging with the wolf as his ideological opposite. Through their "antagonistic cooperation," the pig steps outside his house, passes the point of no return, and begins his engagement with the wolf between the poles. In doing so, he gains the perspective of both ends of the polarities and emerges with the power of each.

Our first inkling of this new thinking occurs when the pig agrees to go to the turnip patch with the wolf at six o'clock in the morning but actually goes at five. This behavior lies outside the realm of customary pig behavior. In choosing to engage the wolf, however, the pig understands that survival requires the use of dimensions contrary to the one side he habitually uses. At this point he begins to seek truth rather that parroting the "right" answers of mother pig.

Another important initiation for the pig has just taken place. He has made inquiry into forbidden territory. He must have questioned himself: "What am I protecting? At what price do I protect? Is this bringing me what I seek?"

By being reflective and self-correcting he brought a new maturity to the examination of his commitment to the values of culture and self-preservation as he understands them. By choosing to reassesses his behavioral and moral precepts he understands with greater purity that only some of his tenets will continue to serve him well. He will come to learn that if he holds his precepts exclusively, he will be developmentally weakened.

His two brothers were choiceless and were consumed by the wolf in that very choicelessness. To the extent that they chose, they were enriched. Their shortcoming was that they did not re-examine their values as they matured.

The third pig began a deeper questioning: "Who am I? What is the purpose of life? How will I achieve it? What is the nature of the relationship between the world and the greater truths that are beyond it?"

To this end, the pig slowly realized that he and the wolf are inextricably linked. Their strong attraction comes from a bond deep in his psyche. The closer the pig gets to integration, the stronger the attraction to the wolf will be; the stronger the attraction, the more the wolf will reflect the pig's deeper self. One way to know when we are working with our dark side is when we just can't stay away from it. It can at times have our whole attention. We are either very attracted to it, or very repulsed by it, but both result in the same outcome – choicelessness.

A woman was raised in a very innocent, upper class, demure fashion. She found herself madly attracted to leather-clad "bikers" who were the antithesis of her upbringing. Whenever she was in a state of low self-esteem, she was compelled to seek them out. Her attraction was fueled in part by her need to shock her mother, that is, reject her value system. It also represented the unlived portion of her psyche, that which was exciting, dynamic, forbidden. She was alternately attracted to and repulsed by both sides of her life, and because she did not examine either, she was choiceless in both.

Life is too powerful for one to go forth in blind innocence, as did the first pig, and too complex to stay the same, as did the second pig. Moving firmly along his developmental path, at first claiming and then becoming trapped in safety, the third pig now takes a step toward transformation by embracing the opposite of his trophy of safety – risk. He is passing into the realm of transformation. He is engaging paradox.

To do this the third pig is taking on life afresh. Not that he is starting over, but his world view is shifting. As an outcome of expanding his world view the third pig questions the security of the brick house, responds to the call to action, and, as a qualified learner, engages the wolf. It is now that the pig begins to realize the comprehensive nature of the wolf's relationship with him: the wolf is here for the pig's learning.

THE TURNIP PATCH

Going to the turnip patch significantly changes the pig because there he begins to claim a fuller self. There the paradoxical sides of himself are revealed and taught. The pig now elects to look at parts of himself that he and his culture have chosen to deflect, toss away, or not acknowledge. In the turnip patch the pig mines the darkness, sorting through the hidden booty for any gold that might have gotten naïvely or defensively tossed in it.

In this sense the turnip patch phase represents the examination of self and the collective. It involves digging up what self (ego) and the collective (culture) bury in the darkness as forbidden or unacceptable.

This examination can happen only when the pig has the courage to challenge the idea that he already has the right answers. Prescribed right answers always have a flavor of a rule: Whatever is permitted is mandatory and whatever is not permitted is forbidden. Prescribed right answers ensure that behavior is mandated and examination circumvented. They allow no choices.

The shadow is our exalted, despised, and feared self which resides in the unlived portion of our being. It holds much value for us at this mature stage of our development. Carl Jung tells us that the shadow is 90% gold. The pig is gaining access to his shadow by mining the unexamined sides of himself symbolized by digging up and nourishing himself on the turnips buried in the turnip patch. In this way he multiplies his choices and expands his power.

Within the pig, as within us, lie many behaviors that are base, untrustworthy, unrepresentative, and unacceptable. Some of them should remain buried. Other behaviors buried in the darkness, however, will prove to become a power rather than an obstacle if guided by the strong hand of maturity, esteemed intent, and ethical behavior. They will serve to nourish the pig and fuel his next steps.

MINING FOR GOLD

A bright, young man had recently graduated with a degree in law. He wanted to be a good lawyer but was troubled because he assumed he lacked the necessary aggression. Through counseling with me, he discovered that he had strong negative feelings about the "macho" image. Throughout his college career, he disapproved of his male colleagues' attitudes and behaviors towards women. As a result, he dismissed virtually the entire range of assertive behavior as unacceptable.

Realizing that he was dis-empowering himself, I asked him to do the Mining for Gold Exercise. I had him list all the assertive behaviors that he would sometimes do, and second, all the assertive behaviors that he would never do. This second list represented a dimension of his shadow. He was now in a dilemma: he identified with one side, but clearly realized the value of some things on the other side of his list. His next task was to examine the list of those things he would never do and choose some he might use on an experimental basis. These I asked him to put in an "I will do temporarily as an experiment" category. After some discussion about this new category, he went off eager to make his discoveries.

After some time, the young man reported to me that he found he could remain true to his values of respect and human dignity while simultaneously being empowered by a new fuller range of human behavior. He did what the pig did at the turnip patch: he embraced the darkness, thus laying claim to a larger share of the continuum. Through courage, careful reassessment, and a growing wisdom, he found ethical power and much needed resources in that which had been buried in the darkness. To identify exclusively with "non-macho" behavior would have caused the whole structure of his success in law to echo hollowly between the walls of mistaken defenses. He would have unnecessarily tossed away behavior that had nothing to do with male dominance. In his second pig stage, he had aped the "right" behavior of his peers and was continually eaten by the wolf through his inauthentic, disrespectful behavior toward women. Later he graduated to being safely imprisoned within his brick house of "non-macho" behavior, but he was troubled and disempowered. After his experiment with aggression he gained greater access to the whole rather than an exclusive identification with only a part.

Another man used the same exercise to great benefit. He wrestled with a problem of being "Mr. Nice Guy" to a fault. It made him fearful of ever hurting anyone with his behavior. Goodness worked to his detriment because he never allowed himself to appear "not good." His "What I Actually Do List" included: compassion, gentleness, love, service, being understanding, and accepting others' bad behavior without complaint. His "What I Fear List" included: narcissism, bullying, physical violence, inducing fear in others, lying, verbal abuse, and demanding good service for himself. His "My Experiment List" included these two: narcissism and being demanding. The one thing he chose to experiment with was narcissism. It soon became apparent that what he wanted was to live his life more for himself rather than solely for others. The resistance came in the form of social pressure from people who wanted him to remain the same. He brought narcissism into his everyday life by doing what he wanted, saying what was on his mind, and letting other people think whatever they wanted to think about his behavior. In noting his anxiety, he realized that his ethics were so strongly skewed toward the good that this new behavior still did not violate the integrity of others. He benefited from the experiment by gaining the ability to set a direction in his life and to stick to it, regardless of others' agendas for him. He did not choose narcissism; he chose the bits of gold hidden in it.

TRICKERY

Let us go back to the trickery of the pig. After carefully examining the old order, he was about to establish a new one. To ensure this outcome, the pig stepped beyond childhood innocence and tricked the wolf.

The use of trickery is actually an ancient method of transformation. In the scriptural story of Jacob and his mother, Rebecca, trickery was used to gain the father's blessing for Jacob although it belonged by law to his brother, Esau. Jacob and Rebecca were successful in their plan, and by their conspiracy, interrupted a centuries-old pattern. As a result of the shift of power through the father's blessing, Jacob's lineage produced the House of David which was the ancestry of Jesus, the Christ. Like Jacob and Rebecca, the pig resorted to trickery in order to enter safely into the realm inhabited by the wolf.

We typically confuse negative with undesirable. In so doing, we are unable to undo or own many projections that could serve us as we mature in life. Instead of befriending and integrating those negative traits, we insist upon alienating and projecting them.

As we gain awareness and power by mining our darkness, however, we must be able to discriminate between that which is useful and that which is not useful. It's important to remember the lessons of the first two pigs. If we aren't choiceful about our experiments, or don't examine our choices, we will only trade one blindness for another and be eaten by the wolf. At the same time, the call to action is imperative and must be followed to establish a new order for ourselves.

The turnip patch gives us more of ourselves than we can imagine. What we have tossed out or ignored may well be influencing us; what we have chosen to embrace may blind us to its shortcomings. But dig in the darkness we must, in order to move on to further engagement with our wolf.

II

THE APPLE ORCHARD

THE NEXT DAY, the wolf returned again to the pig's house. ❦ In a calm voice he spoke to the pig through the door, "Little pig, Farmer Brown has an orchard with scrumptious apples. ❦ This is the perfect time in the season for them. ❦ They are falling from the trees, just waiting for us to pick them up. ❦ Would you like to come apple picking with me?" ❦ The pig said, "Of course. What time shall we leave?" ❦ The wolf replied, "Five o'clock," and bid the pig good day. ❦ The little pig, thinking he would redo the trick from the turnip patch, went to the orchard an hour early. ❦ But it was much further away than he had anticipated. ❦ While he was in a tree picking apples, he saw the wolf loping up the path, coming in his direction. ❦ To his horror, the wolf padded right to the

bottom of the tree in which he sat. ❦ *The wolf drooled in anticipation in spite of himself.* ❦ *Absently licking his chops, he asked in a neighborly fashion, "Are the apples ripe for picking?"* ❦ *The pig stammered, "Y-y-yes, they taste wonderful, too. Here, you must have one."* ❦ *The pig hurled the apple as far as he could throw it. The sweet, red, juicy fruit rolled down the hill, and the wolf chased it as if pulled by an invisible thread of greed. ❦ Taking advantage of this opportunity, the pig jumped down from the tree and scurried home as fast as his chubby little legs could carry him, clutching his prized basket of apples tightly to his side. ❦ He fell into his house and quickly bolted the door against the hunger of the wolf.*

WAY TO GO PIG! Once again he has bested the wolf and is still secure. Using his knowledge of the wolf's behavior, he saved himself, narrowly, by the hair of his chiny, chin chin.

First, in the turnip patch, the pig learned much from his "wolf self." He accomplished this by digging the turnips — uncovering that which had been buried in the darkness — and finding some useful behaviors there. Through the use of experiments, the pig was able to nourish and recreate himself, absorb this "wolf knowledge" and actually apply it to the wolf.

In the apple orchard the little pig had his first face-to-face encounter with the wolf. He hadn't planned to confront the wolf directly. In fact, it had been his hope to avoid direct contact altogether by the same trick he had used before. The trick had lost its effectiveness, however, but the pig understood this too late. In a split second the pig realized his worst nightmare was taking place. He had come eye to eye with the wolf. Now he was forced to face the fear he had been avoiding all of his life. He had to face his own dark side, or else his life would be consumed trying to deny its existence. All this is necessary in the scheme of personal development. From direct confrontation with his worst nightmare — the wolf — the pig will become competent to face an even newer future.

THE WORST NIGHTMARE

What is your worst nightmare? What are the things you find yourself denying or avoiding at all costs? What do you fear more than anything else? Success? Telling yourself the truth? The repetition of your past? Being promiscuous? Becoming responsible for yourself? Being abandoned? Intimacy? Being told what to do? Being out of control? Becoming healthy? Being dependent on someone else? The worst nightmare is not necessarily the worst thing that can happen, like the death of someone close to you; it is an encounter with the part of yourself that you spend your life refusing to engage.

At the apple orchard phase of development our worst nightmare will come loping down the path towards us demanding to be dealt with. We must stay in contact with it long enough to see the next step. Looking through the lens of our denial, our worst nightmare is obscured. In the initial face-to-face confrontation, we see only our fears. At this point we typically run back into old patterns for safety, oblivious to the fact that we are not actually safe, but living instead in a precarious world of denial.

This reminds me of a woman who chose the safety of denial over growth. She did not think much of herself. Her appearance was unkempt and her environment in disarray. She behaved in a scattered, frantic manner that spilled into her professional life. Growing up fearing her own beauty and dynamism, her sensuality and full womanhood became her deep feared shadow. Over time, it became evident that her worst nightmare was that she would become awakened to those qualities and then be overwhelmed by them. Secretly she envied the woman in her shadow and at the same time she despised her. As a result of counseling to save a shaky marriage, she took the risk of allowing herself to become a powerful, sensual, vibrant, successful woman. Soon she found herself right in the middle of her worst nightmare. What did she do? She scurried quickly back into her brick house of defenses by sabotaging her successful business and relationship. She would not tolerate staying in the apple orchard and facing the wolf. Success in this stage of development occurs only when one is willing to stay face-to-face with his or her worst nightmare. Until then, the pig is culpable.

The wolf's initiate may eventually feel guilt or shame and, in an attempt to escape culpability, deny his or her behavior. The denial serves as a paradox and actually crystallizes the wolf, bringing into existence the missing opposite that the initiate refuses to claim. It is in this way that the initiate summoned the wolf into the apple orchard. The wolf is the initiate's own self, making the wolf's appearance inevitable. By the pig's own presence, bidden by his denial, the avoided nightmare inevitably came loping down the path. With unswerving tenacity, the seeker, again and again, brings about his or her own demise at this phase of development. The shame or guilt is projected onto the wolf and he is again made the designated evil one.

From this point on in the story, a more profound level of impeccability is demanded of the pig. The encounter between the pig and the wolf at the apple tree could have ended with the pig being consumed. Through his experiments in the turnip patch, he gained many resources deleted from his awareness by his personal and cultural mother pig. He became aware of some of these resources as he matured in his understanding of the nature of the wolf. Next, he had to act on this knowledge. Although the pig learned about his wolf's compulsive nature, he himself was free of choice-less compulsion. This is symbolized by his willingness to surrender his apple and throw it to the wolf as an offering. When the pig tossed the apple, he knew that the wolf would be pulled down the hill by his greed.

GREED

The compulsive greed of an aspect of our shadow self must be dealt with in all positions of power. When religious, economic, and political leaders, for example, arrive at the apple orchard stage of their development with all its fruits of power, they may not fully realize the import of their circumstances. Attaining this power comes with, among other things, an initiation into service. Invested with the fruits of the community, symbolized by the apples in the orchard, the community's power is placed in the hands of the initiate.

Attaining this power is also a process initiation because the investiture happens over time. If the initiates make their potential real, they find themselves pushed across the boundary to greatness in the eyes of the community.

In the apple orchard, a leader's every wish is treated as a command. Fascinated by what surrounds him or her, the initiate plucks and eats the fruits at will. Yet the wielding of this power and its accompanying opportunities of privilege demands that the initiate be in the process of becoming whole. However, if the initiate has been instinctually, emotionally, or intellectually wounded on their journey and have not healed their wounds, they will find themselves using the fruits of their power solely for themselves as a substitute way to soothe their pain or fear. In seeking satisfaction for their hungers, those at this stage risk forgetting the greater need of their flocks, those they steward, or their constituents. Very clearly, temptation is part of growth. It is a purifier that determines when we have the necessary mastery of stewardship to take our next step.

In our own ways, we are all subject to the same dilemma. We must at some point in our development pass through the orchard having overcome greed and its companion, selfishness. If we are seized, we will either spiral down into earlier stages of growth, or move in monotonous circles until we learn the lessons of the orchard. One of those lessons is that power exists for service.

Only when we are mature and secure enough to release our grip on the prizes of our position and let go of our attachment to the forces we have mastered can we, with our basket still overflowing with powers, leave the apple orchard whole.

Spiritual Awareness

Here the story takes a turn into even deeper meaning; the pig's nature changes, the quest changes, and the role of the wolf changes.

The wolf is teaching the pig his lessons well. The pig absorbed wisdom as nourishment from his teacher in the turnip patch, and demonstrated his understanding in the apple orchard. Now the pig's quest becomes more overtly spiritual, guiding him towards even deeper mysteries. At this turn the pig requires someone more profound than a mentor to guide him. The wolf, aware that he has a qualified student before him, becomes the great teacher. He is now the Merlin, the guru, the shaman initiator, the Hag, the profound guide who illuminates the darkness in order to show its beauty, mystery, and steps to enlightenment.

The pig is finally beginning to understand what's happening to him, and the meaning of life is becoming clear. The relationship between the psyche and the light of self-awareness deepens: wolves eat pigs until they don't! The pig's spiritual learning then dawns: he must change this situation!

Conscious volition emerges out of patterns of instinctual drives. Human development unfolds as the emergence of self-awareness. When we escape symbiotic relationships with instinct, we live with a constant buried fear of being pulled back in, swallowed up in the vast sea of unconsciousness. The pig's relationship with the wolf at the turnip patch is changing this. The apple orchard is the purifying crucible.

SUBSTITUTE SACRIFICE

Historically, ritual acts are performed to purchase safety from the danger of being consumed. Animals are sacrificed to the gods, humans and their substitutes (fruit, unleavened bread, incense) are offered, old men and the community send young men (and now women) off to war.

Substitute sacrifice, in which one object is sacrificed in exchange for another, is a motif common in our myths and, thus, in our politics. Persephone gave Psyche a task requiring her to venture into the underworld. In order to gain safe passport, Psyche tossed a substitute offering of bread to the three headed hound, Cerberus. More commonplace was the European upper class practice of paying for a substitute to take their place in battle. This occurred from ancient times through the American Civil War, and even beyond. Substitute sacrifices are used psychologically in the hope of forestalling annihilation by the forces in the darkness.

The most feared force of all – death – drives most sacrificial offerings. Death is seen as the ultimate triumph of primordial unconsciousness over self-awareness. Life is full of expiatory sacrifices to ward off this inevitable outcome and its foretastes. ("Dear God, if you let me pass this test, I'll be good.") When offerings are made, unconsciousness appears to be temporarily appeased.

In the apple tree, the pig performs just such a ritual while, on the other hand, he readies himself to join the rank of those who defeat death. While the pig throws the apple as a gesture of appeasement, he also consciously lays another claim to his wholeness. He realizes that he no longer needs anyone to be the intermediary between himself and his psyche. The pig has made his own sacrifice, thereby claiming direct connection to the source of life. He is his own priest.

The third pig initiate at the apple orchard is on the way to facing the fear of death again, only at this stage he is equipped with maturity and the wisdom gained from the great teacher.

The pig has entered the orchard, its trees heavy with ripe fruit. He has the proffered apple in his grasp, but rather than eat it, he tosses it down the hill as an offering for the world. In releasing the fruit, the pig makes a sacrifice to substitute for himself. In appropriate primal fashion, the wolf follows the offering down the hill. The pig will later come to realize the even greater significance of this act, namely, the one who eats the apple is the one who gets eaten.

The pig has achieved three great powers in his initiatory experience in the tree. First, he has come to understand the nature of the wolf to the point where he can on occasion, direct the wolf's behavior. Second, by operating consciously in the mysterious workings of the psyche, the pig has claimed for himself the power that has been ceded to the priestly caste throughout history – appeasement of the gods. Third, the pig has consciously assumed the primordial power of the ritual. He is awake to the nature of life. He runs home with a basket full of new power symbolized by the remaining apples. The pig has become the great seeker competent to know great truths.

12

The Fair

Safe at home again, the little pig waited. ❨ Predictably, the wolf was soon knocking at his door. ❨ "My dear little pig," said the wolf, for by now he had grown quite fond of the pig and had begun to respect him through their encounters, "there is a fair taking place in the nearby town. I would like you to accompany me there. Seeing that we have so much in common, I am confident that we would find our travels and companionship most rewarding. Shall we meet here at four o'clock tomorrow morning and go to the fair together?" ❨ The pig said, "That would be delightful," and prepared himself for the next day's journey to the fair, planning, as usual, to leave his house an hour early. ❨ The sun was not yet peeking over the horizon when the pig stole away for the fair. ❨ The wolf, however, had no intention of going. ❨ He sat at home laying plans for the pig's return.

WHAT IS THE WOLF up to now? As usual, the paradox of his role as teacher and devourer is rich indeed.

The pig's awakening of insight at the orchard told the wolf that his student was ready to go to the fair. The fair represents the vast inner worlds full of new ideas, rich spiritual experiences, profound teachings, deep philosophies. The pig is to learn that he is "a traveler, a citizen of two worlds, the inner and the outer."[12] The teacher sends the student to this wealthy environment to deepen his maturity. Because the pig has acquired knowledge, wisdom, and skills through his paradoxical relationship with the teacher, he must now go afresh into these two worlds to penetrate the innermost depths of life that have lain hidden in plain sight.

In this third departure, the pig walks away from his teacher as he had first left his mother and then the brick house of safety. This time, however, he is awakening to his purpose in life. Empowered within his developing awareness of self, he is committed to the call of a conscious future that is interwoven with, and stands on, the shoulders of his past.

This departure signifies another initiation for the pig, a departure from the familiar interaction with the teacher into a new unknown. The pig, however, will leave the wolf only temporarily; once he has explored the fair, he will return to his teacher for further steps in his development.

Going to the fair is finding what has been welded within you. The Celtic mystics call this stage of seeking The Way of the Wyrd.[13] Here seeking is united with solitude, darkness with light, non-self with self. At this point the initiate leaves on a different quest, a quest to discover what the master has been silently installing within him to be aroused later for his enlightenment.

The fair will display all the powers of mind so that the seeker can discover, fetch, and lay claim to what has been welded in him through his interaction with his master teacher. Equipped with a richer self, discovered and matured in antagonistic cooperation with the wolf, the pig is sent into the wealthy learning environment of the fair by the master so as to return as a qualified partner. Because he has awakened the resources to make even deeper sense of the mystery of life, the pig has acquired what in yogic training is called *adikara*, "the right to know" the mystery.

TEACHERS AND TEACHINGS

There is a commandment in the Judeo-Christian scriptures that says, "Thou shalt not steal." One insight to this prescription is germane to our story: "You can't steal what you cannot contain." Developmentally speaking, if we do not have the capacity to absorb a level of growth, it will slip through our fingers like sand clutched too tightly. It will eat us up like the wolf ate the first two pigs. Or it will go the route of the little fathomed greed at the apple orchard. We cannot keep what we are incapable of holding. If someone gets a million dollars, he had better hurry up and become a millionaire so he can get to keep the money. Unless he does, the million dollars will go by the same route that his other money has gone. An ancient yogic teaching says that a fool who falls asleep in front of God will still wake up a fool.

Many levels of teaching are essential for our development, even though they may be difficult, complex, or subtle. In traveling through this maze, a teacher is necessary, especially for the deeper and subtler dimensions of growth. Life provides us with teachers until we are wise enough to become aware of our own. Then, and only then, are we sought out by an embodiment of the true master.

What the true masters hold in common is that they all are wolves; all are committed to our awakening; all show us our darkness and lead us to a glimmer of hidden light, all teach the beauty of the darkness and the mystery of the soul.

Each master has a different knowledge from his or her interaction with life, and gives this "darshana" (point of view) to the initiate. At each pig's stage of growth — from unconscious compliance with the mandates of their legacy, to periodic examination of their assumptions, and finally to having the darkness and the fears it houses become explicitly and plainly projected on another — the pigs were taught.

We can say that each of the pigs' learnings, as well as each of these darknesses, expresses itself as the wolf.

- The voracious devourer who stands guard at the gate is the other side of our frivolous immaturity.

- The wolf who eats up the rigidity of our unexamined life is the other side of our naïveté.

- The wolf who challenges the validity of our defenses is the other side of our arrogance.

- The wolf who invites us to mine our darkness is the expression of all we reject in ourselves.

- The wolf who is our worst nightmare is the expression of our fear of ourselves.

- The wolf who chases the apple down the hill is the expression of our greed and confusion.

- The wolf who sends us off to the fair is the embodiment of our commitment to learn.

All of these wolves are life pushing us into more life.

Maturing to the point of having a competent embodied teacher is a step of great proportion. This teacher is one who has already mastered the student's current developmental stage. Such a one will serve the disciple as the essential correcting mechanism to challenge the student's confusion, limits, and arrogance.

As we saw in the fable, the wolf never intended to accompany or guide the pig through the fair because a proper teacher is now seeking to make the student independent. A teacher of this caliber is rare in the world; rarer still is a fully qualified student. First the teacher examines the student from afar to see if he or she is qualified. The important second step is the examination of the teacher by the student. This examination must prove the teacher selfless. Once the testing has been settled to the satisfaction of both, the student lets go of testing and starts to learn.

In life our wolf nature repeatedly works with our pig nature as devourer in the first and second pig stages. At later dimensions of the third pig stage and into the turnip patch, the relationship moves toward conscious cooperation and begins to take the charge of life away from the benign care of myth, culture, and naïve actions of self-preservation. Our third pig nature begins to claim that responsibility for itself. At this point we also formally choose a teacher, or more auspiciously are chosen by a teacher, and therefore, a philosophy. This is just what happened with the pig prior to going to the fair.

CHOOSING A PHILOSOPHY

A philosophy of life will serve to orient our thinking process and organize our method of inquiry, purpose, direction, and decision making. As we move through the various stages of our developmental structure, we will come into contact with many teachers and their philosophies. A variety of teachings make valuable contributions but, at some point, we will find that we resonate with only one. Eventually it will become important to have one teacher and philosophy so we can resolve the conflicts of method between teachers and teaching styles that will arise. The methods are many; the truth is one.

It is a rare system of philosophy that can tolerate critique. Some philosophies can take a seeker only so far, and some seekers can advance only so far. It is apparent, then, that a periodic critique of philosophy as well as of seeker is an essential self-correcting mechanism. When naming the profound experiences that occur in deeper self-unfoldment, most philosophies wrap their seekers in a strict belief system. By virtue of what they include, they exclude everything else, especially some vital realizations. Periodically revising our philosophy of life as we live it is, therefore, a profound and critically valuable exercise. A theory, no matter how sound, serves us only through withstanding challenges as it and the seeker's understanding matures. Our gods must mature as we mature!

A unique bond has been established between the pig and the wolf. Much has taken place between them that could only happen in the master/disciple relationship (master of self) and (disciplined, sincere seeker). The pig, entering deeper into the complexity of life, will now temper his experience with knowledge gained from the wolf. Let us see how he will make the wolf's wisdom his own.

13

THE BUTTERCHURN

THE LITTLE PIG *was quite late in returning home from the fair.* ❨ *He had purchased a butterchurn there and was carrying it home with him.* ❨ *Pleased with his purchase, he smiled to himself as he strode purposefully along.* ❨ *Keeping his eyes open for the wolf, the pig neared his residence.* ❨ *He stopped on the hilltop above his house and spied the wolf leaning against the tree in his very yard.*

M. McColl

At the fair the pig gained insight into the nature of existence. He moved towards a deeper understanding of the realms of mind in which he lives. His return with the butterchurn represents his accomplishments.

The butterchurn in the possession of the pig is like the trophy that the triumphant hero brings back from a quest. In many myths the hero returns with a trophy that represents the accomplishments of the quest as well as the victory over evil forces. In the *Kathopanishada,* Nichiketa endured his contest with Yama, the King of Death, and returned with a many-colored chain, symbolizing his knowledge of the secret of death.[14] Cinderella likewise endured many trials before dancing at the ball and returning with her glass slipper as a sign of the accomplished woman she had become. So, too, our little pig has endured several interactions with the wolf and is now returning from the fair. He learned much about the perennial questions: "Who am I?" "What is the purpose of life?" "What is the relationship between the manifold universe and the beyond?" And now, he returns with the butterchurn, a talisman representing his attainments.

The butterchurn symbolizes the much-prized faculty of discrimination. Deemed of utmost importance in many spiritual traditions, discrimination is the ability to consciously and skillfully make and unmake boundaries, to see them clearly, and use them in service of the quest. A churn makes boundaries by discriminating or separating cream, milk, butter, and whey – all present in the common substance of raw milk. It makes many products out of one by the motion of the central shaft and paddle. In addition to being a metaphor for making distinctions in life, the churn is a metaphor for the organization of our human psychological and spiritual development.

Ancient Eastern philosophies have a developmental dynamic in the Chakra System that charts phases and stages of psychological and spiritual development by way of social and metaphysical discernment. The word *chakra* is a Sanskrit term meaning "turning wheel." Like the paddle of the butterchurn separating milk, activity bounds consciousness, distinguishes its light, and in so doing confines and grades the substance of mind into basic categories of human behaviors: security, communion, power, unconditional love, compassion, and intuition.

These elements, when awakened and acting in concert, combine to create a variety of developmentally sophisticated behaviors. These elements are like musical chords which emerge as behavior patterns that are solely the outcome of their synthesis and harmony. Like individual notes in a chord played at once, the consonance provides benefits, skills, and powers that none of them can generate individually.

The central shaft and paddle of the churn now in the pig's possession represent his ability to create, animate, and manipulate these distinctive chords of himself. At this point he has knowledge to form the many out of the one, to consciously take potential and make it actual.

By bringing home the butterchurn, our third pig demonstrates that he has the power of *maya*, the power of creation. *Maya* is ma – mother. It is that which makes distinctions, gives birth to a sense of existence, and engenders a sense of experience. It is the power to define, to invent boundaries creating differences, to make a this and a that, an inside and an outside, a subject and its object.

In systems thinking the notion of a definitional boundary and an exchange boundary can help us bring this concept within our grasp. A definitional boundary is a container that gives a sense of identity within its constraints. An exchange boundary is the border across which two identities in a larger identity contact each other through mutual influence. Some sort of change then occurs.

Once the boundary is drawn, *maya* then gives rise to an exchange across the boundary where influence and change can take place on both sides of the divide.

Maya is like the creation of territorial boundaries on a continent. There is only the landmass, yet individual groups draw lines of separation in their hearts and thinking. Villages, cities and countries now exist formulated by a powerful sense of 'we.' We are this! The 'we' creates laws and rules of containment, protecting the container, and seeking exchange across the boundaries of "we in here" and "them out there." The Civil War between the north and south United States happens inside of *maya*. The economic and political forces of containment and control of exchange happened because of the desire to control the definition and exchange across boundaries.

For an individual, *maya* is the containment of the human psyche in which sexuality and gender emerge. There are no sexual distinctions between fetuses until the third month, when the biological sex is set. This makes way for *maya* to construct cultural and social behavioral constraints in the form of cultural definitions and permitted exchanges. Yin and Yang, Sita and Rama, Dick and Jane are sorted out.

Through his understanding of these definitional and exchange boundaries, a middle-aged man came to realize the power of *maya* in his own life. For some time he had been seeking to understand how he could be made in the image of the Creator as he had been taught in his religious training. Understanding came as he watched his fixed patterns unfold in his most intimate relationships. Like waves moving with the constancy of the moon, he would snatch defeat from the hands of victory. In his relationships he identified himself with a fixed story about how women would hurt him when he became intimate with them. He realized that whether the women would reject him or not, he would interact with them in such a way as to create an exchange that would stimulate his anxiety. Aware of everything that would support his insecurity, he would piece his present with the past so he could feel rejected until they left him.

In a stroke of insight he realized that it was he, himself, who made these pictures a reality. He would constrain himself and those he loved, creating images of his own truth, making something that wasn't there, treating it as real and then becoming influenced by what he had created.

The following limerick demonstrates a part of that power:

There was a man upon the stair.
A little man who wasn't there.
He wasn't there again today.
Gee, I wish he'd go away.

Not that what is created is not real! It is true in its own realm. In the greatness of existence it is not fully true. Like the man upon the stair, images demand to be dealt with regardless of their stature. In this way the man, like the pig, understood the complexity of forces that shaped and held his reality together.

Like the third pig on his journey to self-discovery, the man, too, had to go through the turnip patch and apple orchard, then depart for the fair to return with the deep insight and discrimination of the butterchurn. His insight was that he had the power to bring reality into existence. He finally began to understand how he was made in the image of the Creator.

Our pig, with his chakra system in hand, is now creating his own cutting edge. With this power in his control, the pig returns to his teacher, who sits waiting at the threshold of the next turning point in his quest.

14

THE CONFRONTATION

WHAT SHOULD THE PIG do now? ❦ As he stood on the hill, he saw the wolf sitting between him and the door to his house. ❦ Thinking quickly, the pig crawled inside the butterchurn and rolled in it down the high hill. ❦ Faster and faster he went, right up to the startled wolf, who ran out of his path as quickly as he could run. ❦ The pig landed at his own door, leapt out of the churn, and scampered into the house. ❦ Quite pleased with himself, he drew the bolt against the wolf one final time.

THE PIG RETURNED from the fair with a profound insight into his own nature, the nature of existence, and a growing knowledge of the relationship between the two. The insight resounded within the pig. Now, as he continues on his pilgrimage with his master teacher, understanding will continue to emerge into his awareness.

FACE TO FACE CONFRONTATION

The wolf knows that the final confrontation is at hand. He awaits the pig at the foot of the hill to determine if his beloved student has acquired the right for final initiation.

His student passed the initiations of the brick house, the turnip patch, the apple orchard, and the butterchurn. Now the pig must make use of these resources to take on the final quest; the master himself.

A Zen master, Sokei-an, spoke of the necessity of a strong student in order to ensure that the *dharma* (true nature) be passed on. "When a Zen teacher transmits his *dharma,* it is a championship fight. The disciple must knock him down, show him his attainment, knowledge, and new information. Zen still exists because of this iron rule. Before the female hawk will copulate with the male, she flies for three days through the sky with the male pursuing her; only one who can overtake her can have her. The Zen master is like the female hawk, and the disciple is like the male. You must not forget this law."[15]

This point was demonstrated in the television series, *Kung-Fu.* Kwai Chang Caine, a young neophyte in a Chinese Buddhist monastery, was invited to pluck a proffered stone from his master's hand. When Kwai Chang Caine tried to do this, the master quickly closed his fingers over the stone and replied, "When you are able to take this stone from my hand, it will be time for you to leave."

Throughout their relationship, the third pig has desperately tried to avoid engagement with the wolf. The initiation of exchange has always been left to the wolf, making him the carrier of the pig's denied aggression on one hand and the forces for spiritual transmutation on the other. This time the pig has definitely initiated contact. He has put himself in the position of choosing to exchange with the wolf. He has no idea what will occur. Like the fool on the hill he is stepping off the pinnacle into space with no evidence of the outcome. The supreme choice to be without choice, with no recourse to turn back, has occurred. He has sought the wolf, and the wolf will now prepare himself to close in for the final confrontation.

Religions are formed around individuals like this, those who choose to be individual no more. They step beyond themselves into a new greatness beyond their scope. They have been transformed, and what resides in them now is about to be rearranged beyond their ability to conceive. Buddha and Jesus are two examples on a cosmic scale. Theresa of Avila and Martin Luther King reported their experience while many unknown great beings continue to inspire and guide us in these ways.

Something has happened to the pig at the fair and in the assimilation marked by the butterchurn. We can say that his butterchurn encounter serves as the antidote to the pig's avoidance and denial of his active engagement with the truth of his whole self.

In taking the offensive, the pig climbed inside the butterchurn, showing that he has become the embodiment of everything he has learned. The butterchurn itself becomes a crucible in which the base substance of the pig's awareness is transmuted into the gold of self-realization.

There is an old alchemic saying, "It is the crucible, not the fire, that makes the gold." Long ago, when the pig left the brick house to go into the turnip patch, it was as if he made the commitment to stay in the arena of transformation and eventual transmutation with the master, no matter what. His act of climbing into the churn proved the realization of that commitment.

Climbing in the crucible is an act of surrender to transformation. It is an act of submission in strength rather than an act of submission in abdication. Buddha's pointing to the earth as witness to his attainment, Jesus' surrendering statement, "Not my will but thine be done," Martin Luther King's refrain, "I have been to the mountain," Teresa of Avila's "For me to live is Christ, to die is gain," are all acts of surrender to the force greater than themselves.

The third pig has surrendered. His surrender actively released him into his own essential nature. The pig consciously identified himself with the power of the teachings.

With this power he faced the master. The master is the fire of initiation. Their relationship, master and disciple, is destined to produce the gold of the pig's transmutation, the total integration of self.

15

THE MASTER TEACHER

Not to be thwarted, *the wolf picked himself up from the ground, dusted himself off, and continued his relentless pursuit of the pig.* ❰ *Looking for an opening, he climbed atop the house and arranged himself to descend through the chimney.* ❰ *The wolf set his jaw and said to himself, "This day someone will be eaten!"*

THE WOLF IS SHOWING his metal. His commitment is to the pig's awakening. The wolf, as the consummate master, sees the continuous transformation of his student. The wolf is inspired – no, commanded – by his role to seek the victory of the pig.

One initiate tells a similar story. Swami Hariharananda Bharati, when asked about how he became a disciple of a great saint, reported the following.

"I had been pursuing this great sage to initiate me as his disciple for many years. He continuously told me 'No. I am not your teacher.'

So I became a pest to him! I continued to ask for initiation. In exasperation, he made me custodian of an auspicious mountain site. I resigned myself to my lot and began studying with other teachers. None compared to him, but I felt I had to obey.

Years later, he was visiting me at the site and stayed in the upstairs room I reserved for his use only. I was outside, a floor below, when visitors approached to see me. They came and bowed to me. I said to them, 'You are silly to bow before me when the greatest master alive is just upstairs!'

They insisted that I was the one they had come to see. They tried to touch my feet in reverence. I said to them, 'You are foolish to waste your time with me. Let us all go upstairs and sit at the feet of the great one.'

This argument went on for a minute or two. Little did I know that the master was standing on the balcony overhead, listening to everything. I was startled when he suddenly leapt over the balcony railing and landed behind me. I turned to his intense face. His eyes were huge and full of light.

He said, 'Come now! I must initiate you now, this minute!'

I quickly followed him down the hill and received initiation in the forest temple. I stand before you now because of that moment."[16]

Such masters are rare, and even if an aspirant finds one, few students are prepared to receive such a high degree of initiation. Self-effort is the force that draws the divine grace and moves the guru's spirit, in human or non-human form, to light the spark that results in initiation.

The great mystic masters up through the present often use themselves as an offering to provide what is missing or necessary for the advancement of the qualified seeker in their charge. They become the animated shadow of their pupil. We can see this in the mystery of the friendship of Shams of

Tabriz and his student Rumi, the teaching methods of Don Juan with his student Carlos Casteneda, Jesus' presentation of himself for initiation to John the Baptist, Theresa of Avila's friendship with John of the Cross.

Gestalt theory begins to address this concept of use of self, referring to it as presence:

Presence is a special state of being that provides a context against which others flourish and become more fully themselves...Presence is not about style or charisma. Style or charisma asks for attention, admiration. To acquire presence, one must learn many things and then cast them away. To learn presence, one must be willing to have a full sense of self and be willing to give it away. Presence is the acquired state of awe in the face of an infinitely complex and wondrous universe.[17]

This is closely akin to the position of the mystic master with initiates who have qualified themselves by their effort and accomplishments. The wolf, poised at the chimney's opening, is the embodiment of this commitment to the pig's awakening. "Desire does not aim at the failure, but the success of its rival"[18] The wolf as master now has the task of insuring the pig's enlightenment and, in doing so, placing the mantle of accomplishment upon his student.

16

The Offering

Inside the house, *the pig had set a large pot of soup to cook upon the hearth.* ❨ *Smoke from the fire mixed with steam from the boiling vegetables and rose up the chimney.* ❨ *Suddenly there was a loud splash as the wolf descended the chimney and landed in the pot.* ❨ *The startled little pig quickly fastened the pot lid in place so the wolf could not escape.*

THIS IS A VERY determined wolf! While sitting on the roof, he resolved his next step. As master teacher, he determined to bring about the fulfillment of the last stage of the pig's quest — assimilation of the master's truth. At this point of development in the story (and in life) there is no turning back for either wolf or pig. The wolf, being wise and committed, knows that the day must end with the death of one of them. His responsibility as teacher is to bring this about.

The pig must die to all that no longer serves his transformation. The wolf must offer himself in an act of sacrament in service of fueling the student's awakening. Obi Wan Kenobi, in the film *Star Wars,* offered himself to the laser sword of Darth Vader so that Luke Skywalker would take his next steps; Prometheus offered himself for humankind's illumination; Beauty offered herself to remain with Beast so he could return to his real nature. Once in our lifetime some of us, in a single moment of inspiration, become a sacrament in the service of another's well being. Masters eagerly search the earth for a student who is prepared for a lifetime of such love and commitment from them.

The relationship between the pig and the wolf is one of interdependence. They need each other in order to remove the veil between the darkness and the light. Both must be impeccable in their tasks. The wolf must be an impeccable teacher to coach the pig into final assimilation; the pig must be an impeccable student to deliberately stand in the face of the master, in the face of the gods, and become one of them. Others have found that feat virtually impossible. Many have sought to avoid it, looking to religion to mediate on their behalf and render the divine harmless.

If the pig does not succeed in his final initiation, he is bound to be consumed by a prior state. At this phase of his development, that in itself would be a death. His imperative is to win or die, to assimilate or be assimilated. Success is his only option.

The motif of encounter to the death is portrayed often in myth and fairy tale. Ulysses must kill the Cyclops or be killed; Jack must slay the giant and escape down the beanstalk or be eaten; the miller's daughter must destroy Rumplestiltskin by saying his name or suffer the death of her baby daughter. The final imperative against the darkness is not chosen; it is thrust upon us, and there is no escape.

The common, abbreviated version of the Three Little Pigs story that allows the first two pigs to escape death robs us of the catalyst this imperative provides. The shortened form also breaks the connection of failure and learning. Failure provides us the opportunity to reexamine and change our assumptions and position. As Demming says, "The theory of knowledge teaches us that a statement, if it conveys knowledge, predicts future outcome, with risk of being wrong …"[19] To deny failure denies the importance in the encounters the pigs have with the master, with the crucible of relationship, and with the fire of learning.

The modern version of the story eliminates the turnip patch, the apple orchard, the fair, the butterchurn and the pig knocking down the wolf. Instead it leads immediately from the failure to blow the brick house down to the wolf descending the chimney. It eliminates the core meaning of the fable: the relationship between the pig the wolf.

The chimney was always available to the wolf. The wisdom of the wolf to mature his student before descending and proffering upon him the honor of his full presence is a subtle insight that demands to be taken into account. From the brick house on, the wolf has carefully matured the pig. It is their relationship that allows the pig, through the wolf, to become aware of himself, first through antagonistic cooperation and then ending with unity. The wolf has forced a maturing initiate to face himself and when the revelation was not forthcoming from within the pig, the wolf took the roles of the missing parts so that the pig could see (through projection) and then reclaim himself.

The chimney is supremely pivotal, but requires everything that goes before for its power and meaning to be serviceable to us. The act of the wolf's descent down the chimney is core to the presence the wolf provides to the relationship. Out of his own fullness the wolf provides the pig with what is missing and in doing so, the qualified student is made great enough to later assimilate him.

THE DESCENT OF THE WOLF

In accord with the ancient motif mentioned above, the wolf is pressing his student, the pig, to the death. Pursing the pig against his locked door, and finding no other entrance, he presses the pig by descending into the house through the central shaft of the chimney. This pursuit and descent is replete with rich symbolism.

The descent of the wolf down the chimney portrays the descent of high initiation conferred upon the head of the prepared initiate. The gods have always waited to receive the smoke of the sacrificial offerings made to them by the faithful ones. They wait no more; the gods themselves now descend through the sacred smoke. They descend through the awakened mind of the pig, a mind make strong through keen contact with his own projections and the projections of the collective, through finding what has been welded within him, and through understanding and using discrimination. The gods descend to bring the final goal to the faithful pig.

The wolf, likewise, has always waited outdoors for the pig, accepting what the pig would offer. This time, the wolf in the same fashion waits no more. The waiting and the relationship between the two has served its purpose. The wolf now is the embodiment of the pig's initiation. He embodies the descent of grace. He seeks victory for the pig, but knows that the pig must claim it for himself. The pig has become everything the wolf hoped he would become. He has followed all the steps of development and is now on the brink of becoming one of the chosen. Thus he must be pursued.

SACRIFICE

The word sacrifice comes from the Latin *sacraficere*, "to make holy." Now all the elements for sacrifice are ready. The hearthstone and the cooking vessel are composed of the earth; the soup contains water; the flames are the sacrificial fire; the smoke rides the air; the sky embraces space. As the master that the pig emulates descends from the sky, through the smoke, and lands in the earthen crucible that holds the pig's boiling soup, the sacrifice is performed.

17

THE PIG BECOMES A WOLF

T HAT EVENING *for supper, the pig ate the wolf.*

THE PIG NOW DOES the unthinkable: he eats the wolf. In ordinary reality, wolves eat pigs; pigs are not able to hold the opposite idea in their minds. But this is a new realm of consciousness with new truths. This is a realm that brings the pig into contact with life in a radically different way. His mere existence now catapults him into a whole new order where he will participate in an entirely new province of life. The pig is a transmuted being.

When the little pig consciously assimilates the wolf, he also assimilates the wolf's knowledge and power. Like Siegfried, who slew the dragon and sucked its vanquished blood from his fingers, like the hunter who eats the still-warm heart of his kill, and even like the child who consumes the mother at her breast, the pig eats the wolf, taking nurturing and power. Religious rituals likewise symbolically enact the eating of the body of their redeemers in order to acquire spiritual grace and power.

When he eats the wolf, the pig assimilates his demons as well as his nurturer. He becomes a mystic, one who seeks direct experience with the Beyond. He is conscious within and beyond the rest of the community, because as a realized mystic, he has consumed his wolf. He is transmuted. He has become the wolf.

Mystics descend into the underworld in their quest, emerging with themselves as the trophy. They have awakened to their deeper selves. They are now able to embody the complexity of truth – the unreal and the real, the darkness and the light, the mortal and the immortal. Now the pig has journeyed and claimed the alpha of innocence and the omega of maturity.

Our story ends with the pig returning into life with a unique sense of wholeness. Awakened now, and with his shadow integrated, he has transcended some measure of the unconscious collective and individual self. This task has been an extraordinary accomplishment. He embodies the integrated wisdom of mother pig and the wolf and has stepped beyond them. Because of this, the pig has claimed the right to engage the next unknowns in a succession of further unknowns.

Epilogue

THE RELATIONSHIP of pigs and wolves is not a battle. It is the unconditional desire to know truth. It is the willingness to periodically re-examine truth. It is having the courage to face your darkness. It is taking the risk to question your light. It is being prepared to die to that which no longer serves your unfoldment. It is the blossoming into wisdom when you go into partnership with both the light and the darkness as you surrender to divinity.

Afterword

THIS IS AN AMAZING little book! Charles Bates has taken The Three Little Pigs story and has pulled an immense amount of useful information and even knowledge out of it. I knew the story only in its shorter version, and it tugged at my mind from time to time, but I never studied it. Charles did, and I admire three points in his celebration and interpretation of the story.

The first is his discussion of "second pig thinking." We all associate the straw and the sticks and the bricks with ways of protection or styles of building, but he associates those three substances with ways of thinking. "Second pig thinking" amounts to using the same principles in our new project that have clearly failed in earlier projects. We can do that in private life and also in national life. Intervention failed when we tried it in Vietnam, and so we try it again in Iraq. The government's thought in this manner is clearly "second pig thinking." "Third pig thinking" means a radical shift, a kind of leap, trying something no pigs have tried before, and that shift depends on a clearer grasp of the wolf.

The wolf in this book stands for the shadow side of each of us — those dark, greedy, cunning, base, untrustworthy, unacceptable traits. We usually split them off from ourselves and assign them to another person or another country. I remember once asking an experienced old therapist at a lecture how an ordinary person, let's ssay a 40-year-old woman in a small town, could begin to do some shadow work. He said she can't unless she knows the concept of the shadow. That seemed harsh to all of us, and so he added, "There's one more way; if there is some other person in that town whom she absolutely hates, and if she could break eye contact, so to speak, with that person and quickly look down to her left, she would see her own shadow." That's very good. And we know that if there's anything the pig hates, it's the wolf. Following Charles Bates' interpretation of the story, then, the wolf is the shadow of the sweet little pig.

In "third pig thinking," each of us has to have close contact with the wolf. Bates says, "The wolf has behaviors that he uses to be successful; the pig now claims some of them for himself." For example, the third pig tricks the wolf by arriving at the turnip patch one hour early in the morning. Turnip digging is associated with rooting out what is dark and hidden in ourselves, and Bates remarks, "… the pig realizes that he and the wolf are inextricably linked. Their strong attraction comes from a bond deep in their psyches." We could say that the closer each of us comes to our maturity, the stronger the attraction of the wolf to us. This idea is a very powerful rebuke to fundamentalist thinking whether in church circles or in government circles. If Russia for thirty years has been our wolf, then the two of us must have a bond deep in the psyche, and we need more close contact. That, in fact, is exactly what Robert Frost urged when he visited Khrushchev during the Cold War. He told Khrushchev that America and Russia should set up a cultural competition with each other and see who could be best in poetry, in painting, in exploration of space, in philosophy, and so on. In our persona lives when we begin to feel a strong attraction to people we've always hated, we know that we are beginning to work on our dark side.

A third thing I like about Bates' discussion is his unfolding of apparently innocent details. For example, when the wolf comes upon the pig in the apple orchard and the pig finds himself insecurely hidden in the apple tree, he throws a fine red apple as far as he can down the hill. "… and the wolf chased it as if he was pulled by an invisible thread of greed." Bates suggests that the apple belongs to the whole world of sacrifice. Some sacrifices are done to distract the dark forces so one can get home. When the pig later visits the fair, the wolf tries to catch him by going to the pig's house and waiting there for the pig to come back. It turns out that the pig has bought or earned a butterchurn at the fair. Milk contains butter, cream, and whey, all mingled together, and the churn was invented to separate and discriminate between them. The story says that only after the hero's contact with the wolf does he learn to discriminate, to separate the spiritual "butter" from the rest of the milk. The Persian poet, Rumi, writing about 1245 A.D. says:

> Butter is hidden inside buttermilk …
> For a thousand years all people see is buttermilk.
> The butter has disappeared; no one knows where it is.
> At last God sends a churner. He twists the big wooden
>   stick
> Cunningly, he teaches me where my inner one is.
> This milk has been around a long time.
> Don't stop working with it until the butter appears.

CHARLES BATES unfolds a charming detail in this scene of the pig and the churner. When the pig, returning from the fair, arrives on a hill above his house and sees the wolf waiting, he gets inside the butterchurn and rolls himself down the hill. In this way he frightens the wolf from his post at the door. This is a wonderful idea – how the butterchurn helps in the struggle with the dark side.

As the story closes, it becomes clear that the more one works with the dark side, the more it becomes a teacher. Bates' last brilliant stroke in this discussion is to point out that the story ends with the pig's eating the wolf just as a good student eats his teacher. Winston Churchill said, "I've often had to eat my own words, and I found the diet very nourishing." So each of us, when we leave "second pig thinking" with its endless repetition of old mistakes, can find a way to regard our enemy as a teacher, bring him closer in a shrewd way, and finally nourish ourselves by eating all those parts of us that in the first half of our life we threw away.

ROBERT BLY

Footnotes

1   Marie Louise Von Franz, *Shadow and Evil in Fairytales,* (Dallas, TX, Spring Publications, Inc., 1974), p. 7.
2   Nicholas of Cusa,*The Vision of God,* (New York: Frederick Ungar Publishing Co., 1960).
3   Joseph Campbell, *The Hero with a Thousand Faces,* (Princeton, NJ, Princeton University Press, 1968), p. 58.
4   Heinrich Zimmer, *The King and the Corpse,* (Princeton, NJ, Princeton University Press, 1956), p. 48.
5   Murphy's Law comes from the common experience of people in the marketplace.
6   Carl G. Jung, The Portable Jung, edited by Joseph Campbell (New York, NY, Penguin Books, 1976), p. 139.
7   *Summa Theologicae* of Thomas Aquinas
8   Plato, *The Collected Dialogues,* Ed. by Hamilton and Cairns (New York: Pantheon Books, 1961).
9   *St. Paul Pioneer Press, Viewpoint,* Friday, December 16, 1994, p. 15A.
10 A well-known quotation of the physicist Warner Heisenberg.
11 Swami Rama. *The Bhagavad Gita.* (Honesdale, PA, Himalayan Institute Pressm 1985), p. 7.
12 A frequent teaching of Swami Rama in his lectures.

13 Brian Bates, *The Way of Wyrd*, (San Francisco, Harper San Francisco, 1992), p. 168.

14 Swami Rama, *Book of Wisdom: Kathopanishad*, (Kanpur, India: Himalayan International Institute, 1972).

15 Anne Bancroft, *Zen: Direct Pointing to Reality*. (New York: Crossroad, 1979), p. 12.

16 A personal disclosure of Swami Hariharananda to the author.

17 Intimate Systems Program of the Cape Cod, Gestalt Institute of Cleveland.

18 Raymund Schwager, S.J., *Must There Be Scapegoats?*, (San Francisco, Harper & Row, 1987), p. 11.

19 W. Edwards Demming, *The New Economics*, (Cambridge, MA, Massachusetts Institute of Technology, 1994).

Bibliography

Ani, Marimba. *Yurugu*. (Trenton, NJ: Africa World Press, Inc., 1994).

Ashliman, D.L. *A Guide to Folktales in the English Language*. (New York: Greenwood Press, 1987).

Barfield, Owen. *Saving the Appearances: A Study in Idolatry*. (New York: Harcourt, Brace & World, 1989).

Bellah, Robert, et al. *Habits of the Heart: Individualism and Commitment in American Life*. (Berkeley, CA: University of California Press, 1985).

Bharati, Agehananda. *The Light at the Center: Context and Pretext of Modern Mysticism*. (Santa Barbara: Ross-Erickson, 1976).

Bly, Robert. *Iron John: A Book About Men*. (Reading, MA: Addison-Wesley, 1990).

Bly, Robert, ed. William Booth. *A Little Book on the Human Shadow*. (New York: Harper and Row, 1988).

Campbell, Joseph. *The Inner Reaches of Outer Space: Metaphor as Myth and as Religion*. (New York: Alfred Van der Mark, 1986).

Daly, Robert. *Must There be Scapegoats?: Violence and Redemption in the Bible*. (San Francisco: Harper and Row, 1978).

DeMott, Benjamin. *The Imperial Middle: Why Americans Can't Think Straight About Class.* (New York: William Morrow and Company, 1990).

Dossey, Larry. *Meaning & Medicine.* (New York: Bantam Books, 1991).

Dossey, Larry. *Prayer is Good Medicine.* (San Francisco: Harper, 1996).

Eisler, Raine. *The Chalice and the Blade: Our History, Our Future.* (San Francisco: Harper and Row, 1987).

Farrell, Warren. *Why Men Are the Way They Are.* (New York: McGraw Hill, 1986).

Gardner, Howard. *Frames of Mind: The Theory of Multiple Intelligences.* (New York: Basic Books, Inc., 1985).

Gilligan, Carol. *In a Different Voice: Psychological Theory and Women's Development.* (Cambridge, MA: Harvard University Press, 1982).

Girard, Rene. *Violence and the Sacred.* (Baltimore: Johns Hopkins University Press, 1977).

Goleman, Daniel. *Vital Lies, Simple Truths: The Psychology of Self Deception.* (New York: Simon and Schuster, Inc., 1985).

Hagberg, Janet. *Real Power: Stages of Personal Power in Organizations.* (Minneapolis: Winston Press, 1984).

Hall, Edward T. *Beyond Culture.* (New York: Doubleday and Co., 1976).

Handy, Charles. *The Age of Unreason.* (London: Business Books, Ltd., 1989).

Jacobs, Joseph. *English Fairy Tales.* (New York: G.P. Putnam, 1987).

Keen, Sam. *Faces of the Enemy: Reflections of the Hostile Imagination.* (San Francisco: Harper and Row, 1986).

King, Theresa. *The Spiral Path: Essays and Interviews in Women's Spirituality.* (Saint Paul, MN: Yes International Publishers, 1992).

King, Theresa. *The Divine Mosaic: Women's Images of the Sacred Other*. (Saint Paul, MN: Yes International Publishers, 1994).

Lederer, Wolfgang. *The Fear of Women*. (New York: Harcourt, Brace, Jovanovich, 1968).

Maharaj, Sri Nisargadatta. *I Am That*. (Durham, NC: Acorn Press, 1973).

Maslow, Abraham. *Toward a Psychology of Being*. (New York: Van Nostrand Reinhold Company, 1968).

Mills, Charles W. *The Racial Contract*. (Ithaca, NY: Cornell University Press, 1997).

Miller, Alice. *For Your Own Good: Hidden Cruelty in Child Rearing and the Roots of Violence*. (New York: Farrah, Straus, Giroux, 1983).

Nevis, Edwin C. *Organizational Consulting: A Gestalt Approach*. (Cleveland: Gestalt Press, 1998).

Nodding, Nel. *Women and Evil*. (Berkeley, CA: University of California Press, 1989).

Nuernberger, Phil. *From Loneliness to Love*. (Boston: Element Books, 1999).

Nuernberger, Phil. *The Quest for Personal Power*. (New York: Perigee Books, 1996).

O'Brien, Justin. *The Wellness Tree: The Dynamic Six-Step Program for Creating Optimal Wellness*. (Saint Paul, MN: Yes International Publishers, 2000).

O'Brien, Justin. *Walking with a Himalayan Master: An American's Odyssey*. (Saint Paul, MN: Yes International Publishers, 1998).

Pagels, Elaine. *Adam, Eve and the Serpent*. (New York: Random House, 1988).

Pateman, Carole. *The Sexual Contract* (Stanford, CA: Stanford University Press, 1988).

Pearce, Joseph Chilton. *Magical Child Matures*. (New York: E.P. Dutton, 1985).

Peck, M. Scott. *People of the Lie: The Hope for Healing Human Evil.* (New York: Simon and Schuster, 1983).

Perera, Sylvia Brinton. *The Scapegoat Complex: Toward a Mythology of Shadow and Guilt.* (Toronto: Inner City Books, 1986).

Perls, Fritz. *Ego, Hunger and Aggression.* (New York: Random House, 1969).

Reed, Evelyn. *Woman's Evolution: From Matriarchal Clan to Patriarchal Family.* (New York: Pathfinder Press, 1975).

Schaef, Anne Wilson. *When Society Becomes an Addict.* (San Francisco: Harper and Row, 1987).

Schmookler, Andrew Bard. *Out of Weakness: Healing the Wounds that Drive Us to War.* (Toronto: Bantam Books, 1988).

Schwager, Raymund S.J. *Must There be Scapegoats?* (San Francisco: Harper & Row, 1987).

Tiger, Lionel. *Men in Groups.* (New York: Marion Boyars, 1984).

Tillman, James A. *Why America Needs Racism and Poverty.* (Four Winds Press, 1969).

Ventura, Michael. *Shadow Dancing in the USA.* (Los Angeles: Jeremy Tarcher, Inc.) 1976).

von Franz, Marie. *Individuation in Fairy Tales.* (Zurich: Spring Publications, 1977).

von Franz, Marie. *Shadow and Evil in Fairy Tales.* (Dallas: Spring Publications, 1974).

Weatherford, Jack. *Indian Givers: How Indians of the Americas Transformed the World.* (New York: Fawcett Columbine, 1988).

Wilber, Ken. *Eye to Eye: The Quest for the New Paradigm.* (Garden City, NY: Anchor Press, Doubleday, 1983).

Wilber, Ken. *Up From Eden: A Transpersonal View of Human Evolution.* (Boulder, CO: Shambhala, 1983).

Wilber, Ken. *A Brief History of Everything.* (Boston: Shambhala, 1996).

Zimmer, Heinrich. *The King and the Corpse: Tales of the Soul's Quest of Evil.* (Princeton, NJ: Princeton University Press, 1957).

About the Author

CHARLES BATES is a nationally known consultant and lecturer in the fields of organizational development, leadership, and holistic personal development. He is a noted exponent of yoga spirituality and mind-body integration. Currently he is Chairman of the Board of the Gestalt Institute of Cleveland, as well as co-chair and faculty of Gestalt's Organizational Systems Development Program.

His concentration on mind-body interconnections and its application to the chemical dependency field led to his first book, *Ransoming the Mind: An Integration of Yoga and Modern Therapy*. He has also co-authored *Mirrors for Men*.

Bates has been a student and teacher of mysticism for over thirty years as a disciple of the saint, Swami Rama of the Himalayas. He now heads the Institute of the Himalayan Tradition, an international yoga center headquartered in Saint Paul, Minnesota. He frequently conducts organizational and spiritual retreats and workshops on leadership, relationships, personal development, and yoga mysticism.

Books from
Yes International Publishers

By Charles Bates
Pigs Eat Wolves: Going into Partnership with Your Dark Side
Ransoming the Mind: Integration of Yoga and Modern Therapy
Mirrors for Men

By Justin O'Brien, Ph.D.
Walking with a Himalayan Master: An American's Odyssey
*The Wellness Tree: The Dynamic Six-Step Program for Creating
    Optimal Wellness*
A Meeting of Mystic Paths: Christianity and Yoga
Mirrors for Men

By Theresa King
The Spiral Path: Explorations into Women's Spirituality
The Divine Mosaic: Women's Images of the Sacred Other

By Linda Johnsen

*The Living Goddess: Reclaiming the Tradition of the Mother of
    the Universe*
Daughters of the Goddess: The Women Saints of India

By Others
The Light of Ten Thousand Suns by Swami Veda

Soulfire: Love Poems in Black & Gold by Alla Renee Bozarth

Circle of Mysteries: The Women's Rosary Book by Christin Lore Weber

Streams from the Sacred River by Mary Pinney Erickson & Betty Kling

The Yogi: Portraits of Swami Vishnu-devananda by Gopala Krishna

YES INTERNATIONAL also publishes audio tapes on yoga, spirituality, and personal growth.

Call or write for a catalog:
Yes International • 1317 Summit Ave. • St. Paul, MN 55105
651-645-6808 • Order number: 1-800-431-1579
or visit our website for products and order service:
www.yespublishers.com
email: *yes@yespublishers.com*

Institute of the Himalayan Tradition

is a non-profit organization for study and sharing, for education and community.

It offers residential programs, classes, workshops, conferences, and retreats in holistic transformative training that touch daily lives from the mundane to the sacred, from business to mythology.

The core of all spiritual teachings is yoga meditation.

These classes are taught and facilitated by experienced teachers who have, in turn, been taught by others, and they by others, in a direct line of spiritual teachers reaching back for thousands of years.

The Institute of the Himalayan Tradition investigates the essence of spirituality without the necessity for any particular dogma or doctrine.

Private consultations in wellness, yoga, and spirituality are available with the teachers.

Call for information and class schedule: 651-645-1291

Institute of the Himalayan Tradition
1317 Summit Avenue, Saint Paul, MN 55105